CHOSEN FOR DELIVERANCE

"With the well advised is wisdom."

Pastor Tyler Hartman
Agapé Baptist Church/Boarding School
Stockton, Missouri

REL015000: Religion: Christianity

ISBN 978-1-7344467-4-6

All Scripture quotes are from the King James Bible.

Address All Inquiries To:
THE OLD PATHS PUBLICATIONS, Inc.
142 Gold Flume Way
Cleveland, Georgia, U.S.A. 30528

Web: www.theoldpathspublications.com
E-mail: TOP@theoldpathspublications.com

1.0

DEDICATION

With great pleasure, I dedicate the truths in this book to my loving wife Patricia Hartman, Mr. and Mrs. Clemensen and all the boys of Agape Baptist Church and Agape Boarding School in Stockton, Missouri.

Pastor Tyler Hartman
February 2020

FORWARD

All who find themselves reading this book can have miraculous deliverance from the awful chains of sin. God is intensly interested in every person he has created. He can give each of us an extraordinary life that extends into eternity in his presence where you will receive glorious blessings. The blessings can start now by applying God's gift of salvation to your heart as found in Chapter two. Nothing in this life has the power to change the heart except the words that come from God who sent his son to die in your place. There is life changing power available to you to deliver you from all addictions.

You may be struggling with difficult relationships or finding you need help with the storms coming your way, but God specializes in complete victory and deliverance.

The first ten chapters help the reader to build a solid foundation in obedience to the Saviour. The remaining chapters are for the purpose of giving practical counseling on how to have meaningful relationships with God, with yourself and with others.

TABLE OF CONTENTS

TABLE OF CONTENTS

INTRODUCTION

In these lessons are Biblical promises and principles of Scripture that if you apply to your life will make you prosperous.

When you have knowledge of the Bible and use that knowledge for God's glory, He opens the windows of Heaven for His children.

If you learn what you read and live what you have learned, God's blessings will be poured out on you here and now and for all eternity.

All ages can benefit from His Word and all stages of maturity in Christ will grow in God's grace.

Enjoy the journey of the pursuit of the knowledge of God and His holiness.

"WITH THE WELL ADVISED IS WISDOM."

1. The King James Bible

- In order to have the inspired Bible, one must have <u>every word</u> that proceedeth out of the mouth of God. (Matthew 4:4). There is only one Bible, but many versions. We must decide if we want man's word or God's Holy Word.

- Where did the Holy Word of God come from? Psalm 119:89 – The Holy Word of God came from Heaven. When you purchase a version from the Bible bookstore, what you have are empty and powerless words that come from man.

- How long will God's Word last? Psalm 119:89 – God's Word will last forever. We are promised by God that if we read His Holy Word, we will be blessed and empowered in all that we do.

- How did God deliver His Word to us from Heaven? II Peter 1:21 – Holy men of God spake as they were moved by the Holy Ghost. This Scripture is a verification that God used man as His writing instrument to give us Holy Words.

- All Scripture is given by inspiration – inspiration means God breathed. (II Timothy 3:16). God gave His word from heaven to men and now we have the spoken Word to be our rule of faith and practice.

- God's Holy Word is purified seven times. (Psalm 12:6). It would only take one time by God to purify His word. However, when it is purified seven times, God is saying His Word is both pure and complete.

- God has preserved His Word from generation to generation. (Psalm 12:7). There has been a progression that God has used from the beginning with Moses to the Book of Revelation!

- Forty-seven scholars worked seven years before the King James Bible was finished in 1611 under the direction of the King of England. God chose a little boy with no parents living in the palace in Scotland taught by George Buchannon to become God's choice to bring us in Old English His Holy Word.

2.   God's Simple Plan for Salvation

- Romans 3:23 states that all have sinned. Do you realize that you are a sinner? All men are sinners and all men do wrong things because of their sinful nature.

- Romans 6:23 states that the payment for my sin is death (in Hell). Do you realize that all sinners must pay for their sin in Hell? The law of God states that all men must pay for their sin.

- Romans 5:8 states that Jesus paid for my sin on the cross. Do you realize that Jesus paid for your sins? Jesus came to seek and to save us and to pay for our sin with His blood on the cross.

- Romans 10:13 states that if I call on Jesus to save me, He will give me the gift of eternal life. Do you realize that by calling on Jesus to save you, He will take you to Heaven when you die? Heaven is already paid for, but you must decide to ask Him to save you.

Secure Promises That Make Your Salvation Permanent and Forever

- John 3:16 – "For God so loved the world, that he gave his only begotten Son, that whosoever believeth in him should not perish, but have everlasting life." In this verse it is the promise of God that when you completely rely on Him, He gives you life without end.

15

- John 1:12 – "But as many as received Him, to them gave he power to become the sons of God, even unto them that believe on His name." When you receive Jesus in your heart, you are placed by God into His family with power from God.

- I John 5:13 – "These things have I written unto you that believe on the name of the Son of God; that ye may know that ye have eternal life, and that ye may believe on the name of the Son of God." In order to know you are saved, you must realize that it is the living powerful Word of God that saves you forever with no doubts.

3.   **My New Life in Christ**

- In Christ: I am safe, secure, protected, blessed, inheritance, power, and in the family of God. (II Corinthians 5:17). The magnitude of what God has available for His children far exceeds our dreams.

- In Christ: I am a new creature like a new creation of God. God will make everything new. When God uses the word new, He is saying everything old is gone and you will be discovering this new life in Christ for all eternity.

- In Christ: Old things are passed away such as cursing, anger, stealing, rebellion, stubbornness, drugs, and alcohol. These things no longer have a hold on you. Now it becomes your choice to go back to sin or go on to growth in Christ.

- In Christ: All things have become new. You now have new goals, plans, dreams, beginnings, desires, and new hope in Christ about my life. This new life I have is precious and powerful and glorious both here and now and forever.

- There is no other kind of life on earth, but new life that God gives His children.

- Old life does not exist because those who are not saved do not have life at all because God says they are dead.

17

- The value of new life can only be discovered within the truth of God's Holy Word.

4. Real Men Study the Bible

II Timothy 2:15:

- Men are commanded to study. In the process of our study, the Holy Spirit enlightens our spirits with life giving truth.

- Men study to increase their concentration and focus on God's Holy Word. By focusing on the illuminating power of truth, we are protected from a world of wickedness.

- Men study to gain God's approval. All of God's children will stand before the judgment at which time He will approve or disapprove of our life on earth.

- Men study to learn how to be Godly workmen. Work is what gives a man great value to his family and friends.

- Men study to know how to become a man. Boys play and let their imaginations run wild, but men work and control their minds.

- Men study to stand before God in confidence. Every man will give an account of his life to God, but confidence goes to those who know their God.

- Men study to learn how each doctrine fits with all other doctrines or teachings. To properly understand God's Word takes the Holy Spirit and years of searching the Scriptures.

- Men study for God's perfect will for Life! After a search, we find that God's will for me is to have a spirit of thanksgiving as long as I live.

I Thessalonians 4:11:

- Men study to be quiet. Our God wants us to be able to hear Him when He speaks to us and quiet is His voice.

- Men study to learn how to be still. God chose not to speak in the wind, but in a still small voice.

- Men study to learn a state of rest in the land. Our bodies were not made for 24 hours of work, but also for rest and restoration.

- Men study to be free from alarm or disturbance. Our world is full of activity and disturbance, but God asks us to come away with Him.

- Men study to be peaceable. Most men are for war, but God's Word teaches us to go after peace until we have it.

- Men study not to be offensive. Whatever you give away comes back to you in abundance.

- Men study to not excite controversy. Shun vain babblings and words of no value and words that stir up foolishness.

- Men study to be contented, meek, and mild. Godly men who are content and mild are most like Jesus.

- Men study to be calm in a world of stress. Our society is filled with pills or stress, but the answer is never in a pile, but in prayer, thanksgiving, and praying for others.

5.   <u>Concentration</u>

II Timothy 2:15 – The man of God is required to work.

(Study,   concentrate,   focus,   meditate, memorize, read.)

Men who are being used of God have been engaged in varying degrees of these six activities.

- Concentration takes practice and <u>hard work</u>.
  - o <u>Work</u>: You have to shut out all distractions from your mind.
  - o Learning to concentrate requires strong desire.
  - o Learning to concentrate requires strong determination. The person who God blesses with success in all that he does is this man who stays in God's Word day and night.

- Concentration takes a boy from his play to a man who is a hard worker for his family and friends. The young man who cannot be trusted with a job that requires him to work hard is a very serious drag on the rest of the world.

- Concentration is never seen anywhere as that which is <u>easy</u>. Those people who always take the easy way out never understand that this life is a test just before they enter into eternity.

- Nothing that is so valuable will ever come to you without hard work. The men who God uses to bless us are those who are able to function under the most difficulties without quitting their God-given work.

- Those who are successful as men of God have learned the value of hard work. There is no value in laziness, quitting, and giving up because of the challenges of this life, but the value of a man's life as he stands before God will be rewarded in eternity.

6.   The Success of a Servant's Heart

- There is spiritual power in having a servant's heart. There is an enormous amount of baggage most people carry that could be unloaded if they could only grasp having a servant's heart.

- Serve the Lord in fear and trembling with all your heart. (Colossians 3:22; Ephesians 6:5). When you find that in your heart there is a place you do not give God, your observation should be that of fear and trembling, but if not, that is what makes God angry.

- There is spiritual power in giving honor to those in authority over us. (I Timothy 6:1). By giving honor to your parents and all those in authority over you, blessings from Heaven will flood your heart and soul.

- By not giving honor to those in authority, we dishonor and do hurt to both the teachings of God's Word and His Holy Name. (I Timothy 6:1). A great king in the Bible dishonored God and took credit for all God had done for him and God turned him into an animal for seven years.

- There is great power in desiring to please authority. God is pleased with us when we seek to please those who are in charge of us without talking back when asked or ordered to complete a task. (Titus 2:9). Sometimes we feel justified in rebelling against authority when they have a bad attitude, but God says no excuses are accepted by Him.

- There is great spiritual power in being obedient to authority. When you tell yourself you must obey in order to please God, then God rewards that obedience by sharing with you His mighty power.

- We must be obedient when we are given orders by a person who has a bad attitude or a good attitude, no matter how they give us orders. (I Peter 2:18). God wants us to look past how authority lives and realize that their authority comes from God for our protection.

- Spiritual greatness in the Kingdom of Heaven is given to those who choose a servant's heart. (Matthew 23:11). The greatest people we will ever meet are those with a meek and quiet spirit whose main purpose is to serve others.

- The servant who lowers himself on purpose to be humble will be lifted by God and exalted. Nothing is more beautiful and pleasing to God than those servants who on purpose lower themselves in their own eyes in order to trust God for everything.

7.   <u>Confession is the Key to a Clean Life</u>

<u>Confession: I John 1:9 – In this verse is a condition with a promise.</u>

- Confess: Tell God what you did. Name it. Whatever the sin one has committed against God, He will forgive it when you sincerely tell him what it was you have done.

- God is Faithful: God will do what He said. In this verse, God reminds us that He will take care of our sin because of His faithfulness.

- God is Just: Justice demands that sin be paid for. The beauty of God's justice is that we will never be required to stand before God as guilty because our sins were paid for on the cross.

Promise:

- God will forgive my sin because of His justice. It is inconceivable that God's children would not readily forgive others when God's promise is to forgive us of our sins.

- God will cleanse me: make me clean. To be cleansed by the Blood of the Lamb while serving God is a truth we will be examining throughout eternity.

- God will take me from all unrighteousness. There is nothing I can do to be entirely righteous, but to trust God while He applies the righteousness of His Son to my account.

Peace is Power: Philippians 4:6, 7 – Worry, anxiety, depression are all useless.

- Pray about everything. As the children of God, we are bothered by what Satan is doing, by what others are doing, and by what we do, but God will take care of everything after we pray about everything.

- Thank God for everything. When you finally find a person who has a beautiful, thankful spirit, you have found one who thanks God day and night.

- Pray for others: Supplication. Our God is the one God who answers prayer for His children who are in earnest praying for others.

Promise:

- God will keep your heart and mind through Christ in powerful peace. The most powerful way to live on earth in the midst of war is to live in perfect peace in your heart which comes from God.

8.   Baptism

- Baptism is not God's requirement for salvation. Those who confess their sin to God and invite Jesus to save them will be in Heaven enjoying eternal life without having been baptized.

- In order to have God's blessing on your life, you must learn to be obedient and get baptized. God is pleased with that child of God who is obedient by submitting to being baptized by faith in God.

- A Christian who gets baptized is making a public statement that he belongs to Christ and Christ alone. When you stand up for Jesus and allow yourself to go through the waters of baptism, God is pleased.

- We are commanded to be baptized by immersion, not sprinkling as many churches have done. (Matthew 28:19-20). To be baptized any other way than by immersion is to break the power of identification with our Lord's death, burial, and resurrection.

- It is only immersion that is a picture of the Lord Christ's death, burial, and resurrection. (Romans 6:3-5). It is only by our Lord's death, burial, and resurrection that we gain everlasting life.

- Christ is our example that we must follow in the waters of baptism. (Matthew 3:3). When we keep our eyes on Jesus and follow His example, His marvelous blessings follow us all the days of our life.

- The believers in the Bible obeyed the Lord when they gladly received His Word and were baptized. (Acts 2:41). A great church is where you find Bible preaching, souls being saved, and people being baptized.

- In the Bible, baptism took place soon after salvation and shows you are a new creation in Christ. When you get saved and get baptized and begin walking in your new life in Christ, God is well pleased with you.

9.   <u>An Evil Imagination</u>

- Genesis 6:5 – With the flood, God destroyed the world because of their evil imaginations. (Genesis 11:6). What you find yourself thinking is of great importance to you and also to God so do not let the evil in this world control your thoughts.

- At the Tower of Babel, God scattered men because of their evil imaginations. (Romans 1:21, 24, 26, and 28). If what we are thinking was not important to God, He would not have destroyed the world nor scattered man around the world speaking different languages.

- In the New Testament, God gave them over to a reprobate mind because of their imaginations. When you constantly allow evil thoughts, God comes to the place where He gives up on them.

- Without a clean mind and a good conscience, you are open to the wickedness of the world, the flesh, and the devil. If you do not seek God and His righteousness, you will serve the god of this world system who is Satan.

Where are you with your conscience?

- Good Conscience   I Timothy 1:19
    The person with a good conscience can live free from guilt and shame.

- Weak   I Corinthians 8:7

    Your weak conscience causes you to live like the waves of the sea.

- Wounded   I Corinthians 8:12

    The wounded conscience person wears his feelings on his shoulders.

- Defiled   I Corinthians 8:7

    The defiled person tries to do good, but is put down in his own heart.

- Evil   Hebrews 10:22

    The evil person's desires are evil so he does evil things constantly.

- Dead Works   Hebrews 9:14

    The dead works Christian does not enter into the work of God.

- Seared Conscience   I Timothy 4:2

    Our guide and our teacher is the Holy Spirit who comes along by our side to direct our hearts and minds and our conscience. The seared person is no longer bothered by doing evil and no longer convicted about his works of sin.

Our Conscience is Not Our Guide.

10. <u>Questions for Evaluating My Life in Christ</u>

- What Scripture are you living by? When you know what the Bible says and live by it, you are winning against wickedness.

- What is your level of dedication to God on a scale of 1 to 10 (10 being best)? By being honest about your dedication to God, you can improve your behavior.

- Do you have anger, pride, or resentment in you? When any one of these exist inside of you, it is time to clean your heart by confessing it to God.

- Are you getting your work done? God's blessing is always on those who work hard for Him.

- Are you able to forgive those who hurt you? To forgive everyone everywhere all day long is to live in the beauty of God's mercy yourself.

- Do you have a peaceful and joyful spirit? Ask God to give you the fruit of the spirit in Galatians 5:22.

- Are you happy with your behavior? You will always be happy with your life if you live for others.

- Do you plan on living for God? Those who do truly live for God have put it into their daily schedule.

- What do you have in mind to do for God? Everything you do has to start in your mind. First think about what kind of life you want to live.

- Is it your desire to live holy? God calls us to holiness because that is where His highest blessings are found.

- What struggle do you have that keeps coming back? The way to get rid of a sinful habit is to replace it with a Holy habit.

- Do you have a good prayer life? A good prayer life is where God takes special care of His children no matter what happens.

- Do you have a critical or bitter spirit? Nothing in your life is beautiful when you have a bitter spirit.

- Do you think you will go back to your old fleshly habits? Habits are like ruts in the mud so be sure to enlist good ones.

- Are you strong enough to overcome fleshly sin? The answer to this question is no. Until you call on God for help, you are stuck.

- Do you feel that you are 100% forgiven for all your sin? Though it is too wonderful to believe, it is true that God can forgive all your sin because He is faithful.

- What do you feel God is speaking to you about? The sin of procrastination can steal all your power to live Godly.

- Do you feel God is your best friend? The only way you are going to realize God is your friend is to talk to Him often.

- Have you decided to give your heart to God? The heart is desperately wicked and only God can change it for His glory.

- Can you expect to grow spiritually without reading God's Holy Word? It is the living Word of God that makes us strong enough to defeat our enemies.

- Can you expect to love God's power without a serious prayer life? God's power is given to those who love Him and show that love by going to Him in prayer often.

11. <u>Confidence in God</u>

<u>What is God doing in my life now? (Philippians 1:6)</u>. By going to this verse, we find that God's own plan is to keep working in my life until I see His face.

- Building Godly confidence in me. How? God in His own unfathomable knowledge uses His Word, people, this world, and things I know nothing about to perform His powerful work in me to prepare me for Heaven's glory and His presence.

  - o By troubles
  - o By struggles
  - o By problems
  - o By challenges
  - o By hard work

    God literally uses everything to His advantage to present us to God one day soon without blame and without sin.

- God has already started His good work in your life here and now. God started His good work inside of your heart when you gave your heart to Him.

- God is doing His good work in me today. If you are reading this now, He is presently doing His good and merciful work in you preparing you for Heaven.

- God will continue His good work in me. God has promised that He would never leave me nor forsake me. Praise His name. My future is going to be His good work performed in me all the days of my life!

Proverbs 3:5-6

- Trust in the Lord with all your heart. God wants the very best for all His children so He asks us to give our heart to Him obviously for safe keeping because we do not have power to stay close without Him.

- God will direct your life. God wants us to look for Him each day in everything and if we look for Him, we will see Him in creation, in people, and in all our circumstances.

- You have nothing to worry about when you can pray and thank God for everything. (Philippians 4:6-7). In this Scripture, it is our choice whether we want to worry, complain, and fret over each day or pray and thank God for each day. Some people choose to get stuck in stressors and suffer terribly because of their choice. Choose prayer and thanksgiving and life far above this world's problems.

12. Authority

- The final authority over all is our great God who says in Revelation 22:13 that He is the beginning and the end, the first and the last. The most important choice in life to make is to join God in what He is doing in the world and in my life.

- Our God is the Judge of our motives, our actions, our thoughts, and the intents of every man's heart. (Revelation 14:12). Every person who ever lived will either stand before God at the Judgment Seat of Christ or the Great White Throne Judgment.

- God is the one who has placed all that are in authority over us to give order in society and help us live in peace with each other. (Romans 13:1). Those who fight against God's authority will have lives that will be filled with frustration and end in destruction.

- If you rebel or get angry and fight those over you, you are fighting God, who gave them to you for your own benefit. (Romans 13:1). All of what God made for man on earth is for man's enjoyment and happiness even when he does not agree with God's works.

- The man Korah took men and rebelled against Moses so the earth opened its mouth and swallowed them and they perished. (Numbers 16:1-33). This story in God's Word is to help us see how serious God is about those who wickedly fight those who are trying to love and help them.

37

- If you decide to honor and respect authority, God promises He will give you His umbrella of protection all your life. (Ephesians 6:2-3).

- God is so pleased with all those who honor and respect their parents that He promises to pour out goodness and happiness every day as long as they live and then extend that beautiful life because He said He would.

13. <u>Preparation for Prayer and What to Pray</u>

- In everything give thanks, this is the Will of God for you. (I Thessalonians 5:18). The thanksgiving spirit that you seek has the mighty power of God to keep you in God's will even when the whole world is bent on wickedness and evil.

- Praise God for everything. (Psalm 107:8, 15, 21, 31). Four times God repeats His longing for man to involve himself in praising God for His goodness, and wonderful works to us.

- Love God for everything. (Deuteronomy 6:5). The greatest love a man can have is his love for God which affects every cell in his body.

- Give God the glory for everything (Daniel 4:30-37; I Corinthians 6:20). Therefore, glorify God in your body. Example: Nebuchadnezzar praised, extolled, and honored the King of Kings. Nebuchadnezzar had his kingdom, throne, and servants taken from him because he claimed what he had was what he made happen to himself without God's help.

- Confess your sin. (I John 1:9). The quickest, wisest, and best way to put away any and all of our sin is simply by humbly telling God what we have done against Him.

- Pray for knowledge, wisdom, understanding, insight, and discernment. (Proverbs 15:14; Proverbs 2:3). The more you pray, the more

39

power God gives you to overcome wickedness. The less you pray, the more you leave the door open to wickedness and sin.

- Pray for fullness, presence, power, and the unction of the Holy Spirit. (Acts 13:52; Ephesians 3:19; Colossians 1:9; Ephesians 5:18). The Holy Spirit is our guide, teacher, and helper and it is His desire for us to have victory, but we are required to pray for victory.

- Pray for all that are in authority. (I Timothy 2:1-4). That we may live a quiet and peaceable life. It is a little difficult to navigate this life in a world with so much hate and wickedness, but God wants to protect us with a peaceable life if we would pray for those in authority.

- Pray for the peace of Jerusalem. (Psalm 122:5). This prayer for the peace of Jerusalem is not an option, but a loving command by God who knows best for us and our future.

14. How to Stay Close to God

- Disregard emotions, feelings, persecution, complaints, and high and low days. (Phillippians 4:6-8). Both men and women who live by their emotions will never know and experience the beauty of harmony and sweet fellowship with their God.

- Live by a Godly schedule. (II Timothy 2:15). God reminds us that by reading His living powerful Word, we will experience His favor and His blessings. Those who pray 10 minutes may get a 10 minute blessing, but those who pray most of the day get power and blessings all day long. God tells us that at the Judgment Seat we will either be ashamed or approved by our personal study of His Word. Quality time with the emphasis on quality is what each family member needs not some electronic device. In order for you to have spiritual power and love to give others, you must get alone with God often so you can be filled with God's power and goodness.

  - Bible reading
  - Prayer time
  - Study time
  - Family time
  - Personal time

- Get some Scriptures that God has impressed on your heart and live by them all day every day such as Psalm 35:27; Jeremiah 33:3; Ephesians 4:32; I Thessalonians 5:16-18; Psalm 119:165;

Psalm 34:14. When you surround yourself with the presence of God's Word, you will begin to live it and bless others with your knowledge of His Living Word.

- Forget the bad and always tell the good. No one really has to remind us that we are living in a world of wickedness, but it is our choice whether we will pass on the bad or decide to shun the sin and turn to God's righteousness.

- Give love and acceptance to everyone and you will receive exactly what you gave away. (Galatians 6:7). It is precisely what you give to others that you will get from others.

- The will of the Lord is to be filled with the Spirit, quoting Psalms, speaking to myself in Scripture, singing, and praising with joy in my heart, and giving thanks always for all things unto God. (Ephesians 5:17-20). You may want to ask someone how to be filled with the Spirit of God, but haven't asked yet. God is giving you here in the text how it is done. Use the Word, use singing, use praising with joy and giving thanks, and watch what happens in your heart.

- There is mighty power in living by every Word. (Matthew 4:4). Jesus said to Satan, it is written that you must have God's Words to live and nothing else would work to bring us the power to live life.

15. <u>When You're Angry, What Should You Do?</u>

- Confess your sin. (I John 1:9). Get clean again. Retain a strong desire to get clean every day. Unconfessed sin in your day causes you to have a bad day and a bad spirit and is evidence of wickedness in your heart.

- Cease from anger and forsake wrath. (Psalm 37:8). Do not return to your anger. God's remedy for anger is to determine to stop it. Put anger behind you and leave it in your past.

- If I respond to trouble in my life with anger, I have done this foolishly. (Proverbs 16:32). It is the fool in God's Word who said God does not exist, so do not act as if there is no God by holding in anger instead of trusting God.

- The person who controls his anger is a better person than a mighty man because he has controlled his spirit. (Proverbs 16:32). The spirit of anger is a disturbed, bitter, and out of control person who cannot be trusted by God, by others, or himself. So do yourself a favor and rule your spirit with God's help.

- It is knowledge, wisdom, and understanding that helps a man to control his anger. (Proverbs 19:11). Let it go when you are hurt by others or persecuted or blamed for things you did not do because it is Godly to forgive and overlook personal hurt.

- Choose humility over uncontrolled anger. The children of God are instructed to make a right choice and decide to condescend to lowly things and turn from pride and anger.

- Choose kindness, tenderheartedness, and forgiveness because God forgives you. (Ephesians 4:32). In order to be like Jesus, we have no choice but to forgive and act in kindness to everyone we meet every day as long as we live.

- Choose to love rather than hate. Love is that beautiful treatment which everyone desperately needs and longs for as opposed to hate.

- Choose to give, in place of taking. It is said that it is in giving that you keep what does not belong to you while in taking you cannot keep anything.

16. <u>Anxiety Relief Through the Power of Peace</u>

- Peace through prayer. (Philipians 4:6-8). This is the promise of God to keep your heart and mind in peace through prayer.

- Peace through the power of the Word of God. (Psalm 119:165). When you love the living Word of God, great peace is promised.

- Peace through keeping our mind on Christ. (Isaiah 26:3). By focusing your mind on Jesus, you are given perfect peace.

- Peace through saying "No" to sin. (Psalm 34:14). If seeking peace is your life, your desire for sin will be much less.

- Peace through being filled with the Holy Ghost. (Ephesians 5:18). Thanking God, singing, praising, and asking God to fill you with His spirit produces peace in your heart.

- Peace through the Fruit of the Holy Spirit. (Galatians 5:22). By allowing the Holy Spirit to fill you, He gives to you His marvelous fruit.

- Peace through resting in the Lord. (Psalm 4:8). By giving your heart each day to God, you can sleep at night in peace.

- Peace through being spiritually minded. (Romans 8:6). The battle is for who will you allow to control your mind because to the spiritual mind God gives peace.

45

- Peace through living in the Kingdom of God. (Romans 14:17). Who do you serve because God gives peace to those who seek His righteousness.

- Peace through putting all your trust in God. (John 14:27). Whatever troubles you, give it to God and live in peace that comes from Him.

- Peace through being placed in the Body of Christ. (John 16:33). The world is filled with pain, tribulation, and misery, but in Christ we are blessed with peace.

- Peace through faith in God. (Romans 5:1; II Corinthians 5:7). It is beyond me that God looks at us as if we have never sinned.

- Peace through the Blood of His Cross. (Colossians 1:20). Jesus made peace for His children by His blood on the cross shed for you.

- Peace through making Him Lord of my life. (Acts 10:36). When we make Jesus Lord of our entire life, He rewards us with peace.

- Peace through being blessed by the Lord. (Psalm 29:11). Oh how our Lord loves to pour out on His children enormous blessings, including the beauty of peace.

- Peace through Jesus, who is our peace. (Ephesians 2:14). The veil that hung between

46

the Holy of Holies and the people was torn down by Jesus who is now our peace.

- Peace through taking hold of God's strength. (Isaiah 27:5). On purpose I must take hold of God's strength found in His Holy Word and make peace with my God.

- Peace through maturity and righteousness. (Psalm 37:37). The conclusion of a man's life after seeking God's glorious peace.

- Peace: To be right with God, right with yourself, and right with others. By confessing your sin, you can be right with God. By forgiving yourself, you can have peace with yourself. By forgiving others, you live in perfect peace on earth.

17. <u>Stealing</u>

(Joshua 7)

- God's anger burned within Him against the children of Israel when Achan took the accursed thing. (Joshua 7:1). By looking at the examples given to us from the Old Testament, we can see God's attitude about stealing.

- Israel lost the battle because of Achan, who stole a Babylonian garment, two hundred shekels of silver, and a wedge of gold. (Joshua 7:4-5). If you allow yourself to take what does not belong to you, be sure that what follows you is continually losing all your battles in life.

- All Israel had to pay for one man's sinful stealing. (Joshua 7:11). We sometimes forget that everything we do affects others no matter what we have done and certainly when we steal.

- God's penalty for stealing was to burn him with fire and all that he owned. (Joshua 7:15). We may wonder why such a seemingly harsh punishment, but God was sparing many generations of His people by punishing Achan.

- All Achan's family was stoned and burned with fire for the coveting that he allowed to enter his heart. (Joshua 7:21). The starting place before stealing is in your heart when you allow yourself to want instead of being content with what you have.

- Stealing is strictly forbidden. Exodus 20:15 – Thou shalt not steal. God very kindly shows us that we do have the ability to choose not to steal and wants us to make the right choice.

- Stop stealing and start working with your own hands. (Ephesians 4:28). God knows there are things we need and things we are going to want and encourages us to work for them and pay and remain happy in this God given life.

18. <u>Why Am I Here</u>

- It is God's love for me that brought me here to this place at this time. (I John 4:8). Make sure you are in the will of God in the right place because that is the only place where God will pour out His blessing on you.

- While I am here, God wants to fortify my behavior and teach me how to walk with Him. (Proverbs 3:5-6). Life is learning and hearing God speak to you through His Holy Living Word. Be sure to let learning inspire your heart.

- God wants to bless me and reward me as I determine in my heart to seek Him. (Hebrews 11:6). Be diligent in your daily activities; by faith seek God's presence and then watch how God brings you loads of rewards.

- In this place, I must learn not to gripe, complain, or blame others for my sinful actions and ways. If you find yourself in the awful spirit of unrest, complaint, or blame, know that self has ascended to the throne in your heart.

- I must learn to put Jesus first in everything I do and put myself last. (Matthew 6:33). God has promised to take care of all our needs if we give Him first place in everything we think and everything we do.

- It is here in this place that God wants to teach me how to stop my worry, frustrations, and feeling sorry for myself and begin to learn to thank God for everything. (Philippians 4:6-8). Most all of our struggles in life start our downward decent when we no longer thank Him for everything all day long.

19.   How to Choose a Godly Wife

- Pray for the wife of your life. <u>NOW!</u> When you pray for your wife, you are asking God to protect her and keep her safe and serving God wherever she is.

- Never rush ahead of God's will in finding her. God in His mercy allows both men and women to find each other along the journey He has for you.

- God will give your life's partner a love for you. We often live in the fear that no one will want us or care about us, but God takes care of that for anyone who will trust Him.

- Stay in God's will no matter what trials come. Troubles, struggles, birth, and death are all a part of life. We do not fully understand, but thank God anyway.

- Learn to wait upon the Lord, for all God's blessings come to those who wait like a waiter on the Lord. (Isaiah 40:31). Waiting on God means that you find out what pleases Him and then set out to make Him happy with your thoughts and your actions.

- Never touch the girl you are dating unless you want to totally ruin your future with her. Of course the world does not think anything is wrong with unmarried people arousing unholy feelings, but God still knows people better than we know ourselves.

- First date is taking a girl you know is saved to an independent fundamental church service. This kind of church is hopefully where you will hear the truth taught and preached which is your only hope to get free from the world, the flesh, and the devil.

- Pray on every date that you go on without fail. A good marriage is only made possible by putting God in the center of your relationship with her by much prayer.

- Find out on these dates if she loves God, loves her Bible, loves her preacher, and loves her life in Christ. If you find that this lady does not have a heart of love, be sure you will encounter agony of heart you would never have imagined possible.

- If she is a complainer about her life or her pastor, she will complain and nag you for life. In your journey of life you will find that some people find fault with everyone and everything so God have mercy on that person who has to live with her.

- Love is treatment, therefore, observe how she treats her family and friends. It is precisely how you treat people that shows clearly if you have the heart of God who loves everyone.

20. <u>Tattoos</u>

- God commands us not to print any marks on our bodies. (Leviticus 19:28). When God created us, He put within us differences and on the outside, differences that made Him happy and means God is satisfied with how you look and is pleased with your skin.

- It is the command of God to us not to cut out our flesh. (Leviticus 21:5). Our flesh is God's gift to us to be thankful for and to take care of because it is our only way to become His servant and know we belong to Him.

- God purchased our bodies and our souls and spirits with His own sacrifice of His precious blood on the cross of Calvary. Know that at a great cost to God He sent His only Son to buy us back from our sin so we could live with Him forever.

- Our bodies do not belong to us to mutilate, but instead to take care of for His glory alone. As His child, I do not own my body, but God's Son bought me for His special possession so I belong to Him. Praise His name.

- As God's children, we are ambassadors and witnesses for Him and have no right to mar, cut, or write on our bodies. It is unreasonable and unthankful and unwise to even think that we would cut what God made beautiful.

- It is my responsibility to present my body to God because it is reasonable. (Romans 12:1). At the Judgment Seat of Christ, we who are saved will stand before our Creator and answer for what we did to these wonderfully made bodies.

21. How to Win Souls

By showing a person how to be saved, you will be a part of God's loving plan to keep them from going to Hell where they would have to spend eternity.

A. Teach the verse. Take the time to go over each verse.
B. State the point. The point of each verse is listed below.
C. Review. It is the review where you ask the sinner each question to find out if they understand.
D. Make application. The application is where the sinner is encouraged to pray and ask Jesus to come into their heart.

Romans 3:23; Romans 6:23; Romans 5:8; and Romans 10:13.

Teach each verse from your knowledge. State the point of all four verses.

- All have sinned.
- The payment for my sin is death.
- Jesus paid for your sin on the cross.
- If you call on Jesus to save you, He will give you the gift of eternal life.

Review: Ask these questions:

- Do you realize you have sinned?
- Do you realize that you have to pay for your sin in Hell?
- Do you realize that Jesus paid for your sin with His own blood on the cross?
- Do you realize that Jesus will give you the gift of eternal life if you call on Him?

Application:

If we bowed our heads and I were to lead us in a word of prayer and if Jesus would take you just like you are, would you take Him as your Savior? Let's bow our heads. Now, with your head bowed, call out on Jesus – just call on His name, "Jesus." Tell Him that you realize you are a sinner. Ask Him to come into your heart and save you from your sin. Ask Him to take you to Heaven when you die. If you meant what you said, say, "Thank you Jesus for saving me."

22.   The Limitless Power of God's Holy Word

- Use God's Words and watch your life become successful. The power of God's Words are not in the ink that is on each page, but in receiving these Words in the heart and mind and then saying them until you are able to apply them to your life.

- Jesus used the Word of God to defeat Satan while He was being tempted. (Matthew 4:1-4). The more you use the Living Words from Heaven, the more power you will experience.

- God's Holy Word is a light in darkness, a flame of fire, a hammer, a life-giving power, a defense weapon, and sharp enough to discern thoughts and divide the soul and spirit. (Hebrews 4:12). If you do not know it by memory so you can use it, you will have many defeats in your life.

- Use God's Word to save a lost soul from Hell, to encourage those who are depressed, to give life and healing to the brokenhearted. People everywhere you go in your world need the love, the forgiveness, and the uplifting power of God's Holy Word.

- Hide God's Word in your heart to keep you from living in rebellion and sin. (Psalm 119:9, 11). The enticements of the world are very strong, but you are not required to fail or fall into wickedness because you do have a choice you can make for God.

- Use the words of God in praise, in thanksgiving, in keeping your mind holy and without sin. It is only after you have learned how to praise and thank God that you will enjoy the presence of God in your life.

- Read God's Word to increase your faith, memorize it for inner strength, and speak God's Word to defeat the world of the flesh and the devil. Those who plan for success will make God's Word their cherished, every day habit for the rest of their life.

23. <u>If I Choose Not to Be a Soul Winner</u>

- It means I have not followed Jesus. (Matthew 4:19). When Jesus said follow me, He was going to spend three years teaching them to become fishers of men.

- It means I do not believe I have been chosen. (John 15:16). When you got saved, Jesus Himself chose you to carry on the work of telling the gospel to the world.

- It means I did not get wisdom as I was instructed to. (Proverbs 11:30; Proverbs 4:7). Christians who are wise will find a way to reproduce themselves by giving the good news to as many as they can.

- It means I will not shine as God wants me to. (Daniel 12:3). Those who have taken time to lead others lovingly to Christ will have a glow about them in Heaven for all eternity.

- It means I have not obeyed the Great Commission. (Matthew 28:19-20). No one experiences the presence and power of God in this life like obedient Christians do who spread the gospel.

- It means I do not have a heart that God has for winning lost souls to Him. (Luke 19:10). God's love for man is clearly seen in His offer to the whole world to accept the free gift of everlasting life.

- It means that if I do not warn the wicked, God will require his blood on my hands. (Ezekiel 3:18). It may be that the reason God wipes away our tears in Heaven is because we see all the people we should have warned, but did not.

- It means that I do not have the mission of our church to witness with the Holy Ghost's power to the uttermost part of the earth. (Acts 1:8). If we have a love for God as is His desire for us to have, we will love the lost more like He does.

24.   Preaching

Successful Teaching and Preaching (I Timothy 3)

- Ephesians 5:18 – Be filled with the Spirit. Having been filled with God's spirit opens your eyes to what God is saying to you from His Word.

- Many hours of study in the Word of God. After immersing yourself in the Word of God, you will be able to give it to others.

- The message must have moved you before it will move others. Most any audience can tell if God has spoken to you from His Word by how you give it to them.

- Many hours of prayer is the preparation we are in need of to move God's people. When you check on the men of God who have had a powerful influence on others, you will find in them a strong prayer life.

- Walking with God is the man of God's greatest treasure. It is the most electrifying experience that a man will ever know on earth when you walk with God.

- Get all the education you can – at least a master's degree in theology. Men have done less and men have had more education, but nothing is more valuable than being well prepared.

- Soul winning is imperative for God's man. Others will follow your ministry if you are going somewhere, but none want to follow failure.

- Be sure to study administration in college in order to run the business of the church. Pastors have weaknesses just like all of us do, but running a church does need administrative ability.

- Pastoring a church is going to require all your ability and God's power. One of the wisest decisions a young pastor can make is to be a second man before taking a church by yourself.

- Hard work and long hours are required of the preacher in order to be used of God. Yielding to God to preach is far more valuable and higher than becoming the president of any country.

25. The Will of God for My Life

- Teach me and instruct me in the way that I should go and guide me with your eye. (Psalm 32:8). By praying this same prayer to God, it shows Him that you are willing to follow His leading in your heart.

- Not my will, but thine be done. (Luke 11:2). We do not always pray the perfect prayers and by praying this we can be assured safety in God's answer.

- Delight to do God's will. (Psalm 40:8). God knows your heart and when His will is your delight, He sends the Spirit to direct us.

- Teach me to do thy will. (Psalm 143:10). God's will must be found in His Word before you can know it and do His perfect will.

- We know we are in the family of God when we are doing His will. (Matthew 12:50). The joy of being in God's will enhances our everyday life with God's family all around us.

- God's will be done. (Matthew 26:42). The will of God is not always easy, but after you choose it over your own will, blessings flow from Heaven on us.

- Do the will of God from your heart. (Ephesians 6:6). There is a difference between your heart and your mind which means give God your heart to do His will.

- Give God your heart because He knows how to take care of your most precious possessions. (Proverbs 23:26). God tells us that our heart is desperately wicked so keep no part of your heart for yourself.

- Present your body as a living sacrifice. (Romans 12:1-2). God knows that we serve Him in the body He gave us and that body must without fail be given to Him.

- God said He would show you His will for your life if you will seek Him. Without seeking God with all your heart, you will never experience the beauty of your maker.

- "Delight thyself also in the Lord; and He shall give thee the desires of thine heart." (Psalm 37:4). Ask anyone who has walked with God what He does for us and they will verify that He does even give us our desires.

26. **Every Christian Will Come to a Crossroad Decision**

Your Decision

- Just as God brought Israel to view the Promised Land, God will show you a promised land where you will make your decision to trust God or disobey God and wander in the wilderness. God still leaves the decision with us as to whether we choose to follow Him into battle or refuse Him.

- If you obey God and go into the promised land God has for you, He will give you many victories and few defeats. Yes, many are the battles that we will fight, but defeat comes only to those who turn back and quit.

- In the promised land, you learn to live thankful, live praising, live joyful, and live prosperous. (Psalm 1:3; Joshua 1:8). No one is perfect, but how beautiful it is to follow our God and stay in the presence of God's victory.

- When God shows you the promise and you decide to live in the disobedient, selfish lifestyle, you will experience many defeats and failures and very few victories. The land of many victories is for those who choose to live for others.

- Israel decided to rebel against God after seeing the Promised Land, so God sent them into the wilderness for 40 years until they died. (I

66

Samuel 15:23; Joshua 5:6). When God gave us the ability to choose, He gave each one of us within our reach overcoming power for life inside the promises of His Word.

27. <u>Reason Why I Go Back to My Sins</u>

- No fear of God in my heart. The Christian who goes back into his sin does not realize his only power over sin is found in the Word of God.

- No fear of the powerful destruction of sin. Reading about the flood in Genesis should cause us to reflect on the awful devastation of God's judgment on sin.

- No fear of the holy, fierce anger of God. Nowhere but in the Bible do we find so clear a picture of the anger of God on His people for their wickedness.

- No fear of the power of God's judgments. It is the justice of God that demands that sin must be paid for no matter who it is that sins against Him.

- No fear of the consequence of sin. The consequences of man's sin are all around us, but we sometimes choose to sin and fall into a life of useless existence.

- No fear of the power of Satan to take thousands to Hell to burn forever. If we could experience one second of the fires of Hell it would be so bad we would try to save everyone we meet from its consequences.

- No fear of the dreadful destruction of the fires of eternal Hell. Hell is forever a reality we have trouble seeing in our minds, but it is still eternal damnation.

We are commanded to fear God lest He destroy thee from off the face of the earth. (Deuteronomy 6:13-15). All of God's commands in His Word are still a choice each must make for himself whether he fear God or not.

We are obligated to choose the fear of the Lord. Every man must make a choice to serve the god of this world system or the God of glory.

The fear of the Lord must be learned. (Deuteronomy 31:13). It is the duty of every parent to teach the fear of God to their children by example.

In fearing God, we have confidence, hope, and righteousness in our ways. (Job 4:6). When you find yourself in sin, go to God in confession and repent quickly because God hates sin.

Serve the Lord with fear. (Psalm 2:11). Each day of your life all day long make each moment about God, thanking Him, praising Him, and confessing your sin.

He honoreth them that fear the Lord. (Psalm 15:4). We must not seek or even want honor from men, but when God is the one behind honor let it turn to humility.

The Lord is with them that fear Him. (Psalm 25:14). God reveals His secrets to those who choose to fear Him and honor Him and He rewards them with His powerful presence.

28. <u>The Duties of a Husband</u>

(Ephesians 5; Colossians 3)

- God made women to be social creatures. In the heart of most wives they long for their husbands to talk to them and after that to be pleased to just listen while she talks.

- God made women to be helpers and followers. As God's helper, she needs most for her husband to be the spiritual leader he was made by God to be.

- God made women to be taken care of by men. A man who goes to work all the days of his life is fulfilling the purpose he was made for to support his family.

- God made women to follow the spiritual leadership of men, so make sure you know the Bible so you can teach her the Bible. God's requirement for man is to study God's Word and teach his wife and family what God has said.

- Cultivate the atmosphere of Godly love. If a husband will choose to love God and love his wife and family, all those around him will see God in that man.

- Men must develop humility toward his family and friends. Pride in a man is extremely difficult to absorb and live around, but humility draws his wife to him.

- Men must not allow inner negative feelings towards his wife. Wives are treated wickedly by those husbands who entertain bad thoughts about God's gift to men.

- Men must instill value and worth in his wife and children. If your home is to be a place where the wife and children are open to God's Word, you must learn to encourage them often.

- Men must learn to give compliments and praise to their family. As a husband, you will need to learn a whole new vocabulary of positive and reinforcement language.

- Men must treat their family with the Bible love because love is expressed in how you treat others. It is how you treat your wife that she is assured of your love for her and your love for God and family.

29. <u>Bitterness</u>

Acts 8:23

- Sharp dislike in taste or circumstances. All of us know those who have a bad attitude of bitterness by what comes out of their mouths and actions.

- Cruel and severe words that express inner hurt. Those with hurtful vocabulary go everywhere spreading pain and anger like a bad storm.

- Feelings that result in words that inflict pain on others. Bitterness is like a terrible black cloud over all the earth that inflicts wounds on all of us.

- Expressing inner misery with continual complaint. Know for sure that the person whose words hurt others has a broken spirit.

- Holding a grudge with hatred and anger. By holding on to our pain in unforgiveness, we spread evil on all who are around us.

- Having inside of you a severe temper. The longer you act out of an evil uncontrolled heart, the deeper you fall into the rut of no return.

- Feeling no self worth and no real value. Value does not come from achievement or from others around us, value comes from God alone.

- Having deep sorrow along with painful distress of mind. No one hurts more deeply than that person with a bitter pain in their heart and mind.

- An inside rejection of how one has been treated or bad circumstances. Rejection is what we did to Jesus at the cross of Calvary. God help us not to do it to anyone else.

The Gall of Bitterness

- Anything extremely bitter coming from the heart or mind. Let us be aware of hurting others because we have allowed our emotions and feelings to come out of our mouths.

- To fret and wear away by friction one's emotions. (Romans 6:13). To allow worry and anxious fears to run your life means you do not trust God.

- Break the bond of bitterness by yielding yourselves unto God as those that are alive from the dead. When you give everything to God by prayer and thanksgiving, our great God delivers us from the bonds of bitterness.

30. Lessons About the Tongue

- I can keep my life happy in Christ when I speak only words of wisdom. (Proverbs 13:3). Everything in my life is about relationships which means what comes out of my mouth enhances my relationships or destroys my relationships.

- The troubles in my life often come from unwise words out of my own mouth. (Proverbs 34:13). All your words you speak in this life are recorded by God and will destroy you or save your life and those of your family and friends.

- A man of spiritual understanding controls his words so that his testimony is clean and powerful – be not deceived by an uncontrolled mouth. (James 1:26). We seem to think what comes out of our mouth is okay, but God says your life will truly turn out each day by what you think and say.

- If you truly desire a good life, you have no choice but to always speak words of the Bible in righteousness. (I Peter 3:10). If you want a good life, you will be required to keep many things from coming out of your mouth.

- Do not be included as a hypocrite by slander about your neighbor or any person. (Proverbs 11:9). It is inconceivable that a person who claims to be saved would want to destroy his neighbor with his wicked words.

- Put away and dismiss and dispose of all bitterness, wrath, anger, and evil speaking. (Ephesians 4:31). It must not be allowed in us. It always comes to what we choose to do with our mouth that God blesses or we choose to destroy.

- Personal pride destroys both the possessor and the receiver of such evil speaking. (Proverbs 16:18). More people who love God fail in life because of their tongue than many other paths they choose. Choose life, not ways of death.

31. <u>What God Says About Alcohol</u>

- A priest in the Old Testament who drank any alcohol was killed by God. God is showing us His mercy by doing away with that man of God who was showing his approval of alcohol's destruction.

- The word wine in the Bible is used for both alcohol and grape juice. Many a saved person will have their eyes opened when they see the devastation that alcohol has done at the judgment.

- The context of the Scripture can help you to distinguish between alcohol and grape juice. By reading the verses before and after alcohol has been referred to, you will know if God is telling us about grape juice or alcoholic drink.

- Wine makes a fool out of those who drink alcoholic wine. (Proverbs 20:1). Far too many have been deceived by alcohol and have ruined lives which tell the truth.

- Do not go around those who drink alcohol. (Proverbs 23:20). If you want a life blessed by God, do not hang around those who have not heeded the warnings of God about alcohol.

- Alcohol removes reason and wisdom and changes it into anger, sorrow, confusion, and fighting. (Proverbs 23:29). Be sure to check the lives of those people who buy alcohol and compare their lives to those who refuse it.

- Grief and a curse are for those who go back to drinking in the morning and continue until the night. (Isaiah 5:11). Alcohol is a clear cut way to be cursed for failure that you choose for yourself.

- Grief and a curse are to those who give others strong alcoholic drink. (Hebrews 2:15). According to God's Holy Word, if you work in a store where alcohol is sold, you will be a recipient of the curse.

- "Be not drunk with wine!" means no alcohol for the child of God. Unsuspecting thousands have gone against God only to find that being drunk bites like a serpent.

- Alcohol destroys your ability to have self-control. One of the distinguishing differences between the sinners and saints is that God's children can learn self-control.

- By drinking, one is saying to God, "You're not enough for me, I need my own way of escape." There are many ways to try to escape from our challenges, but by choosing those ways we are saying to God you are not my God.

32. <u>How to Succeed by Choosing Godly Friends</u>

- If it is your desire to have a productive, happy, blessed life, make sure you choose your friends with wisdom. God made each of us to need each other; however, it takes Godly relationships to lift you and encourage you in life's challenges. Proverbs 17:17.

- Depending on how you choose these friends, they will powerfully influence your success or failure, your sinful future, or your seeking God future. All it takes to go down the path of destruction is to follow the wrong person into sin without realizing how you got deceived. Proverbs 18:24.

- Choose the very few who have a heart for God, a heart for church, and a strong desire to do God's will and not their own will. It may take a long time to find a faithful friend, but take your time. It's worth more than a nugget of gold. Psalm 119:63.

- Always choose the man of God who has his life set on serving God for the rest of his life. When you make a wise choice, your friend can help you when you are down drawing you closer to God. Proverbs 27:17.

- Do not be fooled or deceived by those who have no respect for authority, no respect for learning, and no respect for the life-changing Word of God. God tells us of a book He has in which He remembers those who fear him and have their thoughts on His name. Malachi 3:16.

- This is your life, do not discard it by thinking you don't need wise counsel. There are no do-overs in life so get Godly counsel if you want to succeed.

33. Spiritual Leadership Destroyed by Lust

I John 2:15-17

- One date in which you had sex got her pregnant and now you must live with your guilt for a lifetime for a few seconds of fleshly pleasure. These statements are in no way aimed at causing hurt or pain, but to save the people who have not yet made destructive decisions.

- One night alone with a girl who does not have enough courage to say "no" makes her pay for a lifetime because now she has AIDS. Too many in our world are living by uncontrolled appetites of the flesh destroying their own lives and the lives of others.

- One decision to marry a girl you do not know and now you have children, but she goes off with another man at her work. Now you are left to try to raise two children by yourself. There are multitudes of children who are being raised by their grandparents or by a single parent.

- I did not know that she had sex with another man until she came home to tell me that she is having an affair with her co-worker. This same story is repeated all over the world with hurt that some are unable to recover from.

- Divorce is worse than death because you are reminded every day that you were ignorant and unwise and broke a sacred covenant of God between two people who thought they loved each other. Far too many pastors and spiritual leaders are being deceived and destroyed in our permissive society.

34. Satan's Music is Opposite to God's Music

- God has a pattern how He has designed His music to sound. God created music for the purpose of praise and worshipping Him.

- Satan has designed his music to be extremely evil. Satan has twisted and tampered with music until most Christians do not know right from wrong.

- Evil music captures your heart and your mind and destroys both. Evil music is aimed at fulfilling the lust of the flesh. I John 2:15.

- Satan's music removes you from your desire to seek God. If you check the lives of the singers of wicked music you will find they die young from drugs and alcohol.

- Satan with his music demands that you become his slave. Satan is a dictator whose chains of sin become harder and harder to break.

- God's music frees you from bondage and slavery and sets you free to live happy, joyful, and satisfied. By putting in your schedule a life of praise, thanksgiving, and singing each day, you will live joyful and satisfied.

- Satan's music destroys your future and becomes so addictive that you want more and more of that music that makes the body feel good. The whole world is going after singers and performers who become famous and make large amounts of money only to find that their lives are useless lived for self.

- Satan's ungodly music dictates to how you will think and act and behave as his slave. The hardest young people to save from a self-centered life are those who Satan has captured with his music.

35. Order of Events of Earth

- Rapture. (I Thessalonians 4:16-18). We who are saved anxiously await the trumpet sound any moment when we meet our Lord in the air.

- Tribulation. (Revelation 6-19). This world has never seen the terrible events that will take place during the seven years of God's wrath on rejecting sinners.

- Armageddon. (Revelation 19). Most all of the world will gather to fight against Israel and against God in this battle that Jesus will win with His bride.

- Imprisonment of Satan. (Revelation 20). Satan will be cast into the bottomless pit for a thousand years while we are free from his evil prison.

- Inauguration of the Millennial Kingdom. (Matthew 25). There were wise servants and foolish servants, yet the wise and the faithful were given the accommodation of well done.

- The Millennial Kingdom. (Revelation 20; Isaiah 11). Satan will not deceive the nations for a thousand years while Jesus rules and reigns for a thousand years with His bride.

- Satan Loosed. (Revelation 20). God uses Satan to find what is in man's heart to serve and obey God or follow the wicked one.

- The Brief Rebellion. (Revelation 20). The last allowed rebellion of Satan is when he is cast into the Lake of Fire and brimstone to be tormented forever.

- Great White Throne Judgment. (Revelation 20). This is the last judgment in which all sinners will be cast into the Lake of Fire which is called the Second Death.

- New Heaven and New Earth. (Revelation 21-22). This is when God says He will make everything new and when the saved are given all things from their God.

- New Jerusalem. (Revelation 21-22). The new Jerusalem will be a fifteen hundred mile square with 12 gates of pearl and 12 foundations of precious stones.

36. <u>Order of Events in Heaven</u>

(During the seven years of tribulation period).

1. Judgment Seat of Christ. (II Corinthians 5:10). It is at this judgment that the Bride of Christ will receive their rewards just like gold, silver, and precious stones.
2. Marriage Supper of the Lamb. (Revelation 19:9). This is when His Bride, the saved, will enjoy a celebration given by Jesus.
3. All saints come back to earth with Jesus on white horses. We are the army of the Lord which follows Jesus upon white horses when He uses the sword of His mouth to smite the nations.

37. **Many Ways to Obtain God's Mighty Power**

- Wait on the Lord and receive strength. (Isaiah 40:31). Ask the Lord what He wants you to do and wait on Him like a waiter in a restaurant.

- The promise of strength. (Isaiah 41:10). God many times promises to give strength to those who trust Him.

- For those who know their God will do great things. (Daniel 11:32). If you know your God, you will be enabled by Him to do great things.

- Strength on the inside. (Ephesians 3:16). It is the Holy Spirit who gives us inner strength by yielding to Him.

- Admitting your weakness allows you to become strong. (II Corinthians 12:9). When a man realizes strength comes from God and humbles himself, he becomes strong.

- In faith we are made strong. (Hebrews 11:33). Faith in God comes from His Word so study it and become strong.

- Promised power by the Holy Ghost. (Acts 1:8). When you allow the Holy Ghost to direct your life, you are strong.

- In God's hands is power and might for all. (I Chronicles 29:12). God is in charge and He alone gives power to His children.

- Power belongeth unto God. (Psalm 62:11). God is the source of all power because He it is that shares His power with His children.

- Power to establish you. (Romans 16:25). Anyone who shows any kind of strength must know that it comes from God.

- God can do anything. (Job 42:2). God is the one who put the sun in space to warm the earth.

- God does what pleases Him. (Psalm 115:3). Find out what God wants from you and then set out to do it.

- All things are made possible with God. (Matthew 19:26). When a man is without God on his side, he is unable to do anything.

- Nothing is impossible with God. (Luke 1:37). God is the creator of all things meaning He will give you His mighty power if you ask Him.

- Connect "all power is given unto me" with "I am with you always, even unto the end of the world." (Matthew 28:18-20). When you set out to do God's will, He will empower you to accomplish great things.

- But ye shall receive power after that the Holy Ghost is come upon you. (Acts 1:8). God gives Holy Spirit power to those who spread the gospel.

- For it is He that giveth thee power to get wealth. (Deuteronomy 8:18). No one on earth has wealth without that which comes from God.

- God is my strength and my power. (II Samuel 22:33). David declares to us that God is our power.

38. Lustful Appetites

- Definition: carnal appetite, depraved affections and desires, unlawful desire or carnal pleasures, eagerness to possess or enjoy. Many strong men of all different positions have fallen into sin because of uncontrolled lust.

- Whosoever looketh on a woman to lust after her hath committed adultery with her already in his heart. (Matthew 5:28). Thoughts become actions and actions become habits that are very hard to break.

- Lust not after her beauty in thine heart; neither let her take thee with her eyelids. (Proverbs 6:25). Our eyes are a gift from God, but if we use them for selfish reasons we destroy ourselves and others.

- This I say then, walk in the Spirit, and ye shall not fulfill the lust of the flesh. (Galatians 5:16). Yield your heart and mind to the Holy Spirit who gives us power over the lust of the flesh.

- The strong desires of the flesh are too powerful for any child of God to deal with – without God's help. If you hold back any part of your heart from God, you will find yourself going back into old sinful habits.

- Lust is often confused with love, it is purely physical attraction and has no lasting value. It is natural to think that if the body wants it then it's okay, but Satan makes lies believable.

90

- Lust is selfish gratification centering on my own need of my body, leaving out the needs of others. I John 2:15-17 – If any man love the world, the love of the Father is not in him. God says it is not possible to be in love with the world and also in love with Him.

39. <u>My Personal Temptations</u>

I Corinthians 10:13

- My temptations are the same ones that others had before me. (I Corinthians 10:13). We often think that our own temptations are more difficult than others have, but God says all of us have common temptations.

- God will not allow me to be tempted more than I am able to handle. In my experience, I have felt at certain times it's more than I can bear, but God says He will not allow it.

- God's faithfulness to me means that He will make a way for me to escape. It may be that in temptation we are not even looking for a way out, but God says look for escape. There is a way.

- When God makes a way of escape for me, I will have His power to go through all my temptations. (I Corinthians 10:13). Just because we are tempted does not mean we have already committed a wicked sin.

- The power to experience Godly success is available to those who walk with God. When you constantly praise, pray, and thank God for everything, your power will increase.

- There are no excuses that I can give to God that would relieve me from responsibility for my sinful behavior. Be sure that you pray for power over the world, the flesh, and the devil because God answers prayer.

- We are not promised a life that is easy, but God will take me through life's trials if I trust Him. This life that we have been given is preparation for eternity in Heaven so prepare well.

40. <u>My Consequences for My Bad Decisions</u>

I John 1:9; Colossians 3:16; Philippeans 3:13-14; 4:8

- <u>Consequences</u>: The result of things I have done that may be in my life as long as I live on earth. Every good and bad decision that I make will affect my future on earth and in Heaven.

- My sin is forgiven by the grace of God because of the blood of the Lamb of God, but consequences remain. The news is filled each day with actions of men that caused them to lose their occupation and their family.

- Make sure you are forgiven by applying I John 1:9. We are not any of us perfect so by confessing your sin to God you can live clean and live forgiven.

- Be responsible for what you have done in the past for that is what men of God do. Each one of us has to live with what we have done, but we can get up again and keep on serving God anyway.

- Your future is dependent on what good or bad decisions you make today. When you make decisions from Godly counsel and wisdom that comes from God, you have enriched your quality of life.

- You can live positive, joyful, and successful no matter what you have done in the past. By relying on God's promise to forgive us, we can navigate our future with confidence.

- The hardest thing about consequences is, "How do I forgive myself?" It is pleasing to God when we stop relying on our feelings and trust His blood to cleanse us from all our sin.

- If God can forgive all my sins, it is okay for me to completely forgive myself. When we stop looking at ourselves and begin keeping our mind on Jesus, victory is ours.

- Minimize all my liabilities so I can maximize all my assets and blessings. It is through Christ that powerful and great successes can be ours.

41. How To Be Motivated

- You will be the same in 10 years from now except for the books you understand and the friends you have chosen. If you commit yourself to God and the purpose He has for you, motivation will be yours.

- Look where you would like to be 10 years from now and readjust your goals to get there. Those who stretch and reach out for improvement do receive the joy of fulfillment and Godly motivation.

- Pray and ask God to inspire you from His Word with what you need to be for Him. (Joshua 1:5-8; Psalm 1). God's prosperity comes after we fulfill the conditions which are to make His Word our delight and stay away from complainers.

- Make sure that you live in a way that pleases God so that without a doubt you know the Lord is with you. (Genesis 39:3). You can be sure that when you daily praise and thank God for everything, He is pleased with your spirit.

- Learn God's Word so well that God prospers you in all that you do. (Deuteronomy 29:9). Motivation by God's Word takes knowing it by heart before you can apply what you committed to memory.

- Seek the Lord every day of your life on purpose with a schedule and with your heart. (II Chronicles 26:5; II Chronicles 31:21). The key to Christian living is to make less decisions by putting Godliness into your daily schedule.

• Whatsoever you do will prosper when you let God's Word live in you, meaning first place in your mind. (Psalm 1:3). The power that is in God's Word can be yours only if you are motivated to obey His word.

• Faith in God is powerful enough to overcome all that is in this world. (I John 5:4; I Corinthians 15:57; Hebrews 11:6; II Corinthians 5:7). Nothing is more motivating to God's child than when he lives by faith in God's Word.

42. The Benefits of Prayer and Fasting

Mark 9:17-29

- When you recognize that you need to be revived spiritually, it is fasting that will put you back on track. In fasting, God knows you are serious about what you want from Him in your prayers.

- When you need God to do something great, normal fasting and prayer is God's answer. Even in 24 hours of fasting and prayer God is pleased to answer and give us what we need.

- When you have a new job to do or an important move to make, fasting and prayer will smooth out the hard times. Change seems to be challenging for most of us, but God opens the windows of Heaven to those who trust Him and move forward.

- If you have a health problem, fast and pray. It is wise to go to God long before consulting a physician about your illness.

- When the disciples could not cast out the dumb and deaf spirit, Jesus said you can if you will pray and fast. We must pray about everything, but some problems require both prayer and fasting before God is moved in our behalf.

- Both health and spiritual power is revived when you pray and fast. We are encouraged to pray for power, but when you pray and fast God gives special overcoming power.

- Be sure when you fast to drink plenty of water. The spirit is willing, but the body is weak and needs plenty of water or you may have a painful headache.

- You can fast (meaning no food) for as many days as you decide you need to. It is not recommended to fast for a long period without the knowledge of how to come off of a long fast.

- The hard things in life can be handled by God if you learn to pray and fast. There is great power available to that person who dares to trust God's Word and receive clarity of mind, spiritual power, and health through fasting.

43. <u>Sowing and Reaping</u>

- Sowing means to scatter seed that will grow into a crop that you can reap or harvest for profit. (Galatians 6:7). There is a very powerful way to live that brings rewards to us in this life as well as in Heaven if we spread the love of God.

- By applying Galatians 6:9 to what comes out of our mouth, it is clear that we either sow love, kindness, and mercy or hate, rebellion, and arrogance. (Proverbs 16:28). Check what it is that regularly comes out of your mouth and change it to God's mercy and love and forgiveness.

- The word *whatsoever* is describing both your words and your actions. Whether good or bad, they come back to you. (Galatians 6:8). Many of us have heard someone say what goes around comes around meaning what you say and do to others definitely will be done to you.

- If you have a bad spirit or a bad attitude toward others, the law of God says others will have the same bad attitude towards you. (Proverbs 22:8). Selfish and unforgiving people have a spirit that comes from a wicked heart of anger and hate which is how others will treat them.

- If you steal, gossip, or put others down, then others will steal, gossip, and put you down. (Hosea 8:7). We must realize that God's justice grinds slow, but a sinful mouth and sinful actions will be judged because sin must be paid for.

100

- Fight and others will fight you, curse and others will curse at you, help and others will help you, be kind and others will be kind to you. (Hosea 10:12).

44. <u>The Judgment Seat of Christ</u>

- Every Christian will give account of everything he has done to God immediately after the Rapture. (Romans 14:12). Our motives, our actions, and our words are held by God and will be judged when we see Him at the Judgment Seat.

- Every idle word that you speak shall be made known to God at the judgment. Words are powerful and helpful or can be critical and extremely hurtful to those we love.

- Every saved man will stand before God. At this time, He will be our Savior and our Judge. What we have done for God will be rewarded like gold, silver, and precious stones.

- It is appointed unto men once to die, but after this the judgment. (Hebrews 9:27). Our appointment with God who is in charge of all men will undoubtedly be a very humbling experience never to be forgotten.

- Behold, the Lord cometh with ten thousand of His saints. (Jude 14). It will be a glorious, magnificent event when we see our Savior with our family in Christ.

- The Lord searches the heart to give every man according to his ways. (Jeremiah 17:10). Our great God loves to reward His children with a good life here on earth and many things beyond our comprehension in Heaven.

- For we must all appear before the Judgment Seat of Christ (II Corinthians 5:10). There is no doubt about it that you must prepare for eternity while you are still in this fearfully made body.

- And, behold, I come quickly and my reward is with me, to give every man according to his work shall be. (Revelation 22:12). Work for Jesus as long as you can and then you will be pleased and prepared to see Him when He comes for His children.

45. <u>Forgiven</u>

- <u>Definition</u>: To overlook offenses, and to treat the offender as not guilty. It is beyond description the joy of having been forgiven. Now give forgiveness to others for God's gift to you.

- Who forgiveth all thine iniquities; who healeth all thy disease. (Psalm 103:3). With over 8,000 promises in God's Word, our lives can be very beneficial to all of our friends and relatives.

- But there is forgiveness with thee, that thou mayest be feared. (Ezekiel 18:22). There is a great freedom to the person who lives forgiven and then offers forgiveness to others.

- In whom we have redemption through His blood, the forgiveness of sins, according to the riches of His grace. (James 5:15; Ephesians 1:7). Words alone cannot fathom the depth of the riches of God's grace, but will be revealed to us in a glorified body in eternity.

- Much more than, being justified by His blood, we shall be saved from wrath through Him. Romans 5:9 – Justified – Right standing before God. The powerful blood of the Lamb of God is applied to your account when you call on Jesus to save you.

- We are redeemed by the precious blood of Christ, as of a lamb without blemish and without spot. (I Peter 1:18, 19). When God sent Jesus to the cross, He paid for our sins past, present, and future.

- Who His own self bare our sins in His own body on the tree, that we being dead to sins should live unto righteousness: by whose strips ye were healed. (I Peter 2:24). Sin no longer has a hold on your life because your sin has been paid for in full by Jesus' sacrifice.

- Who gave Himself for us that He might redeem us from all iniquity, and purify unto Himself a peculiar people, zealous of good works. (Titus 2:14). We are certainly a peculiar people who choose to live unto God, not to live in wickedness.

46. <u>Identify the Kind of Spirit You Have</u>

- An excellent spirit was found in Daniel. (Daniel 5:12). When God's spirit is allowed to rule in your heart, the change is beautiful to God and to us.

- A talebearer revealeth secrets; but he that is of a faithful spirit concealeth the matter. (Proverbs 11:13). We are not required to tell everything we know to others as some are destroying their friends with their loose tongue. A faithful spirit does not spread bad news.

- Better it is to be of a humble spirit with the lowly than to divide the spoil with the proud. (Proverbs 16:19). Choose humility of the spirit like Jesus showed when he said, Father, forgive them for they know not what they do.

- He that is slow to anger is better than the mighty; and he that ruleth his spirit than he that taketh a city. (Proverbs 16:32). In a world of frustration it is a rare and beautiful find to experience a person who rules his spirit.

- A merry heart doeth good like a medicine; but a broken spirit drieth the bones. Broken spirit means, "I give up; I quit." When your spirit does what God's spirit wants done, its result is medicine to the soul.

- The spirit of a man will sustain his infirmity; but a wounded spirit who can bear? (Proverbs 18:14). Who hurt you or what hurt you? David said, "O God, renew a right spirit within me." (Psalm 51:10). David had committed a sin against God and needed to repent and asked God to help him renew his spirit so he could walk with God again.

- Yield your spirit to God's spirit and He will light up your spirit with the fruit of the spirit. (Proverbs 20:27; Galatians 5:22). Those who have given everything to God can have a life that is so beautiful that it takes nine powerful words to describe.

47. **Stubborn**

- The ship <u>stuck</u> fast and remained unmovable. (Acts 27:41). If you are stuck like this ship was stuck, you will want to ask the God who made you to make you free.

- Samson was stuck grinding at the mill because he was <u>stubborn</u> in his lust for a woman. The chain of sin does get harder to break until you go to God for help.

- If you are stuck, be sure to check yourself for the wicked tick of <u>stubbornness</u>. A tick is able to embed itself into your flesh and make you very sick, but God can change stubbornness to surrender if you are willing.

- <u>Rebellion</u> is the twin brother of stubbornness, so if you have one of them, the other is close by. God said rebellion is just like the sin of witchcraft and puts rebellion alongside one of the devil's main objectives.

- For <u>rebellion</u> is as the sin of <u>witchcraft</u>, and <u>stubbornness</u> is as iniquity and <u>idolatry</u>. (I Samuel 15:23). God hated it when His own people turned to idolatry so He scattered them all over the world for that sin.

- A <u>rebellious</u> and <u>stubborn</u> son who would not obey was brought before the elders of the city to be stoned to death. (Deuteronomy 21:18-21). It may seem harsh to us that God would put down this sin by death, but in so doing He was sparing His people from the awful consequences of sin.

- God refused to allow His chosen people to watch a young man in his <u>stubbornness</u> because He wanted them to <u>hear Him</u> and <u>fear Him</u>. Stubbornness travels like a disease or a plague that could infect generations and God wants us to be delivered from destruction.

48. <u>Who Am I In Christ?</u>

- I am a child of the King of Kings. No one on earth could possibly come close to understanding how marvelous it is to be chosen by God.

- I am my Savior's friend and co-worker on earth. What a faithful friend He is to us who walk with our loving Savior and serve Him each day.

- I have been purchased by His blood. I am God's purchased possession purchased by His blood on Calvary for all eternity.

- I have been grafted into the family of God. God chose the Jews, but when His own people turned Him away, He offered the Gentiles His gift of eternal life.

- I have direct access into the throne room in Heaven by the Holy Spirit. This beautiful gift of access into the throne room in Heaven is given to His children who go there to pray and praise Him.

- I am forever free from being condemned. (Romans 8:1-2). I will never be condemned for my wickedness and my sin because Jesus set me free.

- I know that all things work together for good to those who love God. (Romans 8:28). The tremendous and powerful truth is that for those who love God, He turns everything to good.

- I can never be separated from my God who loved me and gave Himself for me. (Romans 8:35-39). Disaster and war are all around us, but God keeps us and holds us in His hand forever.

- I have been chosen to be a living Bible on earth and God's representative. (Acts 1:8). Everywhere I go and everything I do I must realize that I may be the only Living Bible others may read.

- The Holy One has made my body God's temple. (I Corinthians 3:16). The Holy Spirit, the third person of the Trinity, does not live in the church building, but lives inside of me.

- I am confident in God's great work carried on through my life. (Philippians 1:6). I have confidence in God because I am made in His image. I am fearfully made, and my confidence is in my God to carry out His good work in me.

49. <u>The Consequences of Laziness</u>

- Every man's work shall be made manifest: for the day shall declare it, because it shall be revealed by fire; and the fire shall try every man's work of what sort it is. (I Corinthians 3:13). God makes His work man's work if that man is doing God's will.

- Be not a forgetful hearer, but a doer of the work. This man shall be blessed in his deed. (James 1:25). The kind of work that God wants us to do is clear to those who study and perform what they have heard.

- The desire of the slothful killeth him; for his hands refuse to labor. (Proverbs 21:25). If you have no work to offer to your God at the judgment, all of what you did will be burned like wood, hay, and stubble.

- That ye be not slothful, but followers of them who through faith and patience inherit the promises. (Hebrews 6:12). Lazy and slothful servants are a drag on society and require others to take care of them and do their work.

- The sluggard is wiser in his own conceit than seven men that can render a season. (Proverbs 26:16). Those who never learn that life is work have no idea that their own conceit has destroyed their usefulness.

- Be ye steadfast, unmovable, always abounding in the work of the Lord, forasmuch as ye know that your labor is not in vain in the Lord. (I Corinthians 15:58). The work we do for God and by God in this life will be rewarded throughout eternity.

50. How to Make Your Parents Proud

- Make a schedule specifying times that you will pray, read, study, and meditate on the Bible. By making yourself a schedule that includes prayer, church, and study of God's Word, you relieve yourself from making wrong choices.

- Schedule times to seek work each day until you find a job. Every man is useless to God and himself until he finds what it is that he is made by God to do.

- Look in the phone book for an Independent Baptist Church and attend Sunday school, the main service Sunday morning, the Sunday evening service, and the Wednesday evening service. If you choose the wrong church, everything the rest of your life can turn out wrong.

- Volunteer for all work that the pastor needs done. By choosing the church that God tells us about in His Word, we enter into God's will and become useful to our preacher.

- Be accountable to your parents for your time away from home and all your decisions and actions. The worldly philosophy of doing as I want and what pleases me misses the wisdom that God gives through Godly parents.

- Above everything you do, stay close to God, close to your parents, and close to your pastor with frequent talks to each one. God through

114

Jesus is a gift as parents are a gift and pastors are all gifts from God to keep us from the world, the flesh, and the devil.

- Before making any decisions, clear it with God, your pastor, and your parents. Those who make decisions without Godly counsel destroy their opportunities in pride and conceit.

51. How Do I Treat God's Anointed Preachers?

- I must not stretch forth mine hand, raise my voice, or have any critical thoughts against God's anointed. (I Samuel 24:6). When God hears you complaining or gossiping about the man of God, He allows you to destroy your own future.

- Do not listen to a single accusation against any preachers. I Timothy 5:19 – Accusation means to accuse. If someone in your church comes to you accusing the man of God, tell him that he is God's man, not your man to complain about.

- The angels which are greater in power and might do not accuse others. (II Peter 2:11). The angels in Heaven would not dare to enter into such wicked behavior as accusations against any preacher.

- Accusing others brings God's judgment back to you. Romans 2:1-2 – "Thou condemnest thyself." You may think you are criticizing and complaining about others, but God says you are condemning yourself.

- Obey them that have the rule over you, and submit yourselves; for they watch for your souls. (Hebrews 13:17). Your never dying soul is the most valuable God given possession you have so learn obedience to those in authority.

- Remember them which have the rule over you, who have spoken unto you the Word of God.

(Hebrews 13:17). Preachers and teachers and Godly friends deserve your love, your prayers, and your support.

- God is in charge of putting kings, presidents, and preachers into office. (Daniel 4:17, 25, 32). It may not appear to you to be that way, but God is in charge and you can be sure He will take care of you.

- Dare not to speak against His appointments or His appointed kings, presidents, or preachers. We have become an opinionated people who think it is our privilege to share it with others about those in authority, but to God it is sin.

52. <u>Foolishness</u>

- <u>Foolishness</u>: Void of understanding, weak in intellect, unwise, silly, vain, sinful. Disciplining a child is for the purpose of helping that child's growth into manhood.

- A child is tied to silly, unwise, vain, and sinful behavior. The child who is left to himself will have a struggle in both relationships and in maturity.

- Fathers have the responsibility to use the paddle or rod to correct their children to keep them from a useless life of sinful and foolish behavior. God's ways may not be understood by our general society; however, it is His way that actually makes a man out of a boy.

- A common sinful behavior in most children is their inability to control their tongue, their actions, and their thoughts. This transformation to learn self control takes patient training and love by preachers, teachers, and parents.

- If a child was not corrected by his father, he will find himself doing useless, silly, and sinful things when he should be responsible for his behavior. There is always hope as long as someone will take the time to connect emotionally with the child by consistent Bible training.

- The child who did not learn character, discipline, and responsibility must now learn from God's

Word that foolish and sinful behavior is unacceptable to God and must be changed. The rod that God is talking about is loving and definitely positive reinforcement from his parents.

53. **Persecution**

- The disciples went away happy and rejoicing that they were counted worthy to suffer <u>shame</u> for His name. (Acts 5:41). Jesus suffered unmercifully for us on His way to Calvary when the soldiers nailed our innocent Savior to the cross.

- We must make a decision to suffer with the people of God instead of being pleasured by sinful desires for a small period of time. (Hebrews 11:25). God tells us that we cannot be in love with this world of pleasure and still love our God at the same time.

- Suffering is a part of God's plan to make you perfect, give you a strong foundation, strengthen you, and settle your heart. (I Peter 5:10). The most mature Christians you will ever meet usually are those who have suffered many losses.

- There is a special reward and wonderful blessing for that person who is criticized and persecuted. (Matthew 5:11). All the soldiers in the army of God can expect battles, but God says He will fight for us and then reward us.

- When you serve God with all your heart, leaving home and family members only for God's glory, your reward from God is promised to be the maximum blessing a hundredfold. (Matthew 19:29). God is constantly watching us and quick to help us and give rich blessings.

- The sufferings of this present time are not to be compared with the glory which shall be revealed in us. (Romans 8:18). If we only know what glory God has prepared for all those who suffer persecution in this life.

54. <u>Nothing to Fear</u>

- God chooses to pour out blessings on us all throughout our lives no matter what takes place. (Genesis 26:24). Those of us who have trusted Christ enter into the promises that were given to Abraham, Isaac, and Jacob; so fear not.

- God promises to supply us in all conditions of our world economy, even when supplies become scarce. (II Kings 6:16). God has always provided for His children in difficult times when they call on Him for help; so fear not.

- God has decided to provide protection for all His children when our enemies are at their strongest. (II Kings 6:16). The forces of evil are no match for multitudes that are in the army of God; so fear not.

- It is his promise to us to strengthen, to help, and to keep us with His right hand. (Isaiah 41:10). Fear has torment and those who choose to live in fear have not yet learned to take God at His promises; so fear not.

- God claims us for His own possession even during our most difficult trials. (Isaiah 43:1). The level of difficulty that we face may cause us to doubt, but God has already won the battle; so fear not.

- God assures us that we are of great value to Him and that He knows every detail about us. (Matthew 10:30). God has already put into your

122

future a plan that cannot be changed that you are promised victory; so fear not.

- God reminds us that He is entirely able to handle anything that might bother us, even death. (Revelation 1:17). There are many fear nots in God's word that cover every stage of life so do yourself a powerful favor and fear not.

55. <u>Mocking the Man of God</u>

II Kings 2:23,24

- Elisha the preacher was on his way to Bethel when little children came and mocked him about his bald head, so he cursed them in the name of the Lord, and there came forth she-bears and killed 42 children. The picture that we clearly see in the Word of God teaches us that it is dangerous to criticize the man of God.

- If you mock the poor or those less fortunate than you, God says you have mocked Him and you will be punished for it. (Proverbs 17:5). When God's people take it upon themselves to speak degrading words against the poor He considers it against Him.

- When you look to mock your father and hate to obey your mother, God says the ravens shall pick out your eyes and the eagles will eat them. (Proverbs 30:17). Consider your thoughts and your words about your parents because they are God's gift to you.

- Mockers are defined by their own ungodly lusts and will increase in the last times. (Jude 18). It is too easy to follow in the same pattern of those who have no respect for God, for parents, and for those in authority.

- <u>Mockery</u>: means to ridicule, to scorn, imitate in contempt, to laugh at, to defeat, to disappoint, to deceive, to fool, or vain imitation. Let it not be in the mouth of God's people to in any way mock the preacher or each other.

- When you mock anyone, you are making a fool out of that person and all people are made in the image of God. Oh how beautiful it is to God when God's people love each other, encourage each other, and strengthen the man of God.

56. <u>Promotions</u>

- King Nebuchadnezzar was changed into a beast for seven years "to the intent that the living may know that the Most High ruleth in the Kingdom of Men." (Daniel 4:17). This great King and what happened to him most definitely shows that all men must give God the glory due His name or suffer the consequences.

- God is in charge of all promotions, both small and great. Promotions such as kings, presidents, governors, preachers, jobs, and all others are in God's hands. (Daniel 4:25). It was after the king gave God the glory for His kingdom that God then promoted him from beast to king.

- The kingdom of men belongs to God, making God the one who is in charge of lifting up men and promoting men in every area of life. (Daniel 4:32) All of our presidents and all of our government officials saved or not were given their respective offices by the King of Kings, our great God.

- If it is your desire to be used by God, you will have to remember what King Nebuchadnezzar <u>had to learn</u> when God made him a beast for seven years. He learned to give God the glory. (Daniel 4:37). In God's history book, the Bible, we see that one of the most valuable lessons any man could learn in this life is to give God the glory for everything.

- God promotes those who give glory to Him, praise Him, thank Him, and love Him. If you want to be more like God and less like the beasts of the field, you will need to honor and glorify God each day of your precious life.

57. <u>Cursing and Taking the Lord's Name in Vain</u>

- The person who takes the Lord's name in vain according to God becomes guilty for it. (Exodus 20:7)

- The person who swears according to God's Holy Word can fall into condemnation for what he has said. (James 5:12)

- The person who curses his father or mother shall be put to death. (Exodus 21:17)

- Moses said, "Whoso curseth his father or mother, let him die the death." (Mark 7:10)

- For the sin of their mouth God said, "Consume them in wrath, consume them, that they may not be: let them know that God ruleth." (Psalm 59:12-13)

- As he loveth cursing, so let it come unto him: as he delighted not in blessing, so let it be far from him. (Psalm 109:17)

- There is no fear of God in the eyes or in the heart of the mouth full of cursing and bitterness. (Romans 3:14-18)

58. <u>The Terrible Sin of Sodomy</u>

- Men with men and a woman with a woman is against God and against how God created us. (Romans 1:24). There are a few events in the Bible that have brought down God's wrath on men, but sodomy in Sodom and Gomorrah brought those cities total destruction.

- It is against nature for men and women to change the natural use into sodomizing lust for each other. (Romans 1:26-27). One of God's greatest gifts to man is a woman who gives him children and family and help for his life. To reject this gift in favor of same sex incurs judgment of lethal proportions.

- The man or woman who turns to unnatural relations have rejected God in their knowledge. (Romans 1:28). God puts inside of man a need for God and then shows him all creation with beautiful order everywhere, but man chooses the kind of rejection that brings down God's wrath on him.

- God reminds us that if we turn to uncleanness through lust to dishonor our bodies between ourselves, He will give us up. (Romans 1:24). The choice is ours to make whether we will choose God's way or our sinful ways. No one is born a sodomite.

- Three times God says He will let us have our own sinful desires to serve the creature more than the Creator. (Romans 1:25). We now live in a world where society has turned to the worship of the human body and when that kind of behavior takes place, God lets them have what they want.

- When God says He will give them over to a reprobate mind to do those things which are not convenient, it means to be abandoned to wickedness and eternal destruction. (Romans 1:28). No one has ever found any remains of those two cities where the people chose to dishonor God by dishonoring their bodies.

59. There is Great Value in Seeking Wise Counsel

- Moses listened to the wise counsel of his father-in-law Jethro who said, "this thing that thou doest is not good." (Exodus 18:17). Even the most spiritual among us need wise counsel in order to live a life that brings pleasure to God.

- David's counselor, "was as if a man had inquired at the oracle of God," both with David and with Absalom. (I Samuel 16:23). One would think that David who wrote most of the Book of Psalms was close enough to God not to need counsel, but not so.

- Solomon, King David's son, had advisers or counselors to help him make wise decisions in his kingdom. (I Kings 12:6). The wisest man who wrote the Book of Proverbs also was wise enough to have counselors.

- God says where no counsel is, the people fall. Our falling is often due to attitude about Godly counsel that we can do things on our own. (Proverbs 11:14). Pride takes us away from God and also away from counselors while depending on God draws us to listen to wise counselors.

- If you want to live safe from a wicked world, you must seriously seek counsel from God, His Word, church, and Godly men. (Proverbs 11:14). The foolproof way to failure is to completely rely on your own understanding how this world works.

131

- If your life falls apart, you can trace it back to all the counselors you refused to listen to. (Proverbs 15:22). At the Great White Throne Judgment, men who have rejected Jesus will be sent to Hell for all eternity to recall all those who tried to warn them.

- Disappointment always follows the prideful spirit. Make it a priority all the days of your life to go after wise counsel and you will never have to worry about failure if you listen and act on what you were told.

60. Tongues in the Bible, Literal Foreign Languages

Acts 2

- Speaking in an ecstasy, in unintelligible words, or in languages known only to God came from the heathen world. The deception is so strong that when you hear the truth it's hard to believe you have been taught wrong.

- Mistakenly, Christian scholars, sometimes not very spiritual, have read this heathen meaning of the ecstatic utterance of tongues into the Bible. The overrated speaking in a spiritual tongue that some think comes from Heaven comes from the heathen many years ago.

- In Bible cases where tongues are mentioned, it is literal foreign languages. The Corinthian church known for its worldly practices misused this unspiritual practice of so-called speaking in tongues.

- Tongues in Acts 2 is a miracle of hearing so that people would get saved out of every nation under Heaven. Satan's habit from the beginning has been to put a lying twist to what God says so that his priority of confusion is perpetuated.

- Speaking in foreign languages is not an evidence of the baptism of the Holy Spirit as some churches claim. If you desire the power of God on your life for daily victory, ask God for His power and yield yourself to the leading of the Holy Spirit.

- The baptism of the Holy Spirit does not mean jabber in tongues as often taught. The human mind can be coerced into a kind of speaking that does not make any sense and when that takes place be sure to leave the premises.

- The baptism of the Holy Spirit is God-given power to do His work of saving the lost and building Christians in His world. If you want to see the Holy Spirit in action, find a person who regularly wins the lost and copy that kind of behavior.

61. You Are Not a Victim if You Are Saved by the Blood

- Not one child of God is victim of anything in this world. (John 3:16). Those of us who have invited Jesus into our hearts have been chosen for the greatest gift ever to be given.

- You are not a victim of parents who may turn their back on you or hurt you deeply. (Psalm 23:1). There is nothing that the saved person needs that our great God cannot provide meaning He will take care of all your needs.

- You are not a victim when you lose your ability to walk, to speak, or to see. (Romans 8:28). Our God is so good that He takes what we think is bad and turns it into good in ways we don't even understand.

- You are not a victim of Satan's plans or traps because God has a good work for me to do. (Philippians 1:6). If you place your life in the God who made you, He gives you a confidence that no one can take away no matter what happens.

- You are not a victim because Jesus gave you power to become His own son. (John 1:12). No one is more protected or blessed or loved than the sons of the living, glorious God of Heaven and Earth.

- You are not a victim because God holds you in His hand. (John 10:28). It is literally impossible to take the child of God out of the hand of almighty God, Creator of Heaven and Earth.

- You are not a victim because God knows the way that you take and the choices you make. (Job 23:10). All the challenging trials and testings in this life that I go through make me stronger until I become perfected and beautiful like pure gold for my God.

- God has great plans for us that we have not yet seen or heard if we love Him and keep His commands. (I Corinthians 2:9; Jeremiah 33:3). What God has waiting for us in Heaven is so magnificent that our minds are unable to receive its beauty.

62. Backsliding is Easy

(In Hebrews, God shows us a better way.)

- The easy way to begin backsliding is to simply neglect the Word of God. (Hebrews 2:3). There is tremendous spiritual power in the Words that come from Heaven to keep us from falling into Satan's traps.

- When you begin to doubt God and have trouble believing Him, your heart is starting to harden. (Hebrews 3:8). A wise course of action that each believer must take is to give your heart to God at the beginning of each day.

- God was so grieved with His people for 42 years so they could not have rest in the Promised Land because of their disbelief. (Hebrews 3:19). There is a marvelous rest to those who know they have continued in the will of God with a sincere thankful heart.

- God said to the Hebrew Christians in the Book of Hebrews that because of their immaturity and their dullness of hearing, many things could not be given to them. (Hebrews 5:11-12). Daily miracles should be experienced by those who have made their hearts and minds to carefully listen when God speaks through His Word.

- God's desire for His people was that they would inherit the promises, yet some were slothful and this would keep them from claiming the promises of God. (Hebrews 6:12). The promises in God's Word are for those Christians who live in His Word and let His Word change their habits.

- He that despised Moses's law died without mercy because they sinned willfully after receiving the knowledge of the truth. (Hebrews 10:26-28). This is God's loving warning to His children that when we deliberately disobey His Holy Word, we sin against the Holy Spirit.

63. The Purifying Truth of God's Word

- By trusting God and placing our faith in Him, there is a purifying process that takes place in our heart. (Acts 15:9). God's Word has power to draw us to Him for peace and power and for cleansing us from all sin.

- When you obey the Word of God, the Holy Spirit begins purifying our souls. (I Peter 1:22). The sweet Holy Spirit is our teacher and our guide to open our eyes to pass on to others the love He gave to us.

- Young people are encouraged to change the way they live by applying God's Word. (Psalm 119:9). Spiritual cleaning for the heart and mind of men can only come from those words that God breathed from Heaven.

- We are to be set apart unto God and cleansed by the washing of ourselves in the water of His Holy Word. (Ephesians 5:26). No one can really live without the process of cleansing that takes place in the heart and mind of those who know the value of the Voice of God.

- When we look for Jesus to come back for us with anticipation and hope in Him, God says it purifies us, even as we are pure. (I John 3:2-3). What a delightful hope and joy we have in us that soon we will be like Jesus, the one who makes us pure just like He is pure.

- Because of the many promises in the Scriptures, let us cleanse ourselves from all filthiness of the flesh, perfecting holiness in the fear of God. (II Corinthians 7:1). It is said that there are over 8,000 promises in God's Word given to us who dare to say no to the world, the flesh, and the devil.

64. Relationships

- I must treat all the people in my life with love and respect. My entire life is made of the people God lovingly sends me from the cradle to the grave.

- My entire life will be defined by my relationship with God, my family, my friends, and my co-workers. I must pay special attention to those I meet in this life because everyone of them are gifts to me from my King.

- Depending on how I treat people is how I will be treated the rest of my life. (Galatians 6:7). It is impossible to treat people poorly and with anger to think it's okay with God because you will receive what you gave others.

- God says that when I love the brethren with a pure love that comes from God, He purifies our souls. (I Peter 1:22) We must learn how to look for the good in others treating them with love and respect no matter how we are treated.

- Without loving relationships, I have become nothing and useless to God. (I Corinthians 13:2). How in the world could this be that my whole life would be worthless and good for nothing until I learn how to love God's kind of love.

- God tells us to live a life of kindness, tenderheartedness, and forgiveness because God has forgiven you. (Ephesians 4:32). Love and forgiveness are undoubtedly winning the combination which makes us more like our God.

- The second commandment after loving God is to love our neighbor just as much as we love ourselves. (Mark 12:31). God's gifts to you are your friends and neighbors who need you to care for them like God cares for you.

65. A Lying Tongue

- God hates a lying and a false witness who speaks lies. (Proverbs 6:16-19; Proverbs 12:22). We are constantly bombarded in a world of lies and deception all around us. Let us not be a part of it, but separated from it.

- Ananias and Sapphira lied to God when they sold their property for one price and told Peter a different price and God killed them both for lying. (Acts 5:1-5). The father of lies is that old dragon the devil and his influence is powerfully felt on earth, but the sin of lying brings the destruction of death.

- God says that all liars shall have their part in the lake which burneth with fire and brimstone, which is the Second Death. (Revelation 22:15; Revelation 21:8). These people in these verses have lived that which characterizes their habits of wickedness because they are following their god, the god of this world, the Devil.

- Satan was a murderer from the beginning who has no truth in him, for he is a liar and the father of it. (John 8:44). If you let him, he will take from you all happiness, peace, and joy of life and leave you with emptiness and hate.

- If you have the habit of lying, you must willingly submit to God, placing yourself under God's authority. Resist the devil and he will flee from you. (James 4:7). For each child of God it is a choice that we make to indulge in sinful wicked

143

habits or choose those habits which draw us closer to God.

- In order to stop the habit of lying, you must overcome the evil one with the power of God's Holy Word. (Matthew 4:1-4). Words are extremely powerful especially those words that come from the mouth of God which will defeat the evil one forever.

66. The Goodness of God Leadeth Thee to Repentance

Romans 2:4

- Surely goodness and mercy shall follow me all the days of my life: and I will dwell in the house of the Lord forever. (Psalm 23:6). The goodness of God surrounds us everywhere and yet some Christians can't seem to see it because their eyes have been darkened by sin.

- I had fainted, unless I had believed to see the goodness of the Lord in the land of the living. (Psalm 27:13). Let your heart be fully persuaded. The blessing of spiritual eyesight comes from believing every Word of God.

- Oh how great is thy goodness, which thou hast laid up for them that fear thee. (Psalm 31:19). The beautiful music of the soul is being able to see the goodness of God in your past, your present, and your future.

- He loveth righteousness and judgment: the earth is full of the goodness of the Lord. (Psalm 33:5). Every morning sunrise and every evening sunset and all that lies between is none other than God's goodness to man.

- Why boastest thou thyself in mischief, O mighty man? The goodness of God endureth continually. (Psalm 52:1). In all of eternity there is this great

145

truth that is promised forever and it is that God is good to you.

- We shall be satisfied with the goodness of thy house, even of thy holy temple. (Psalm 65:4). God's house is a place where the people of God go to refill their tanks with enough fuel to last the whole week long.

- O taste and see that the Lord is good: blessed is the man that trusteth in Him. (Psalm 34:8). The ability to taste food that is delicious and satisfying comes from God as well as having the vision of His goodness to live by and thereby repent of all our sins.

67. <u>My Expectations</u>

- My expectations can cause my uncontrolled anger. In a world where most people are driven by their feelings and their emotions, it is useless to expect to be treated with love and acceptance.

- I get angry because I have unfulfilled expectations. Your expectations are your own understanding of life and how it should unfold, but God says you must trust Him if you want to be blessed.

- If I have many expectations that have not been fulfilled, I become disappointed with myself and others. The most difficult person I have to live with is myself. If I can't be at peace with me I will be at war with others.

- When I am disappointed with others, I become upset about life in general and blame others for my problems. If we do not keep our eyes on Jesus, our example, we will look down at some people and look up at others and begin to blame them for our problems.

- When I blame others, it keeps me from taking responsibility for my own actions. The growth and maturity that takes a boy into manhood means that he has learned how to take full responsibility for his mouth and his actions.

- I do not deserve God's mercy and grace which He has given to me by His glorious power. What every man really deserves would be too terrible for the human language to describe because it is punishment in Hell forever, but praise be to God for taking my place at Calvary.

- If I do not deserve His gifts, I must learn to be thankful for everything that He has blessed me with. I must be forever thankful to God for anything and everything that comes to me.

- It takes examining my own heart and understanding my own responses to deal successfully with my anger. The heart of men is terribly wicked so without reservation give your heart to God and replace anger with thanksgiving.

68. Christian Men of God Fail

- If a man fails to make thanksgiving his primary attitude towards God, he will lose all other blessings that God wanted to give him. (I Thessalonians 5:18). It is living in the will of God that ought to be every man's desire especially because it is a simple choice all of us can make by giving thanks to God.

- If a man fails to study God's Word, he cannot have God's approval on his entire life. (II Timothy 2:15). When we stand before God at the Judgment Seat of Christ, we will be held accountable for what we did with God's Living Words.

- If a man fails to take spiritual leadership over his home, he fails to be a man. (Deuteronomy 6:4-10). The kind of leadership God expects from his men is following Jesus and teaching the Bible to his family by example.

- If a man allows his wife and children to push him around, he may live in fear of his own wife instead of his fear of God. (Ephesians 5:21). The man who walks with God will not have a problem with submitting to his wife and then in turn she will learn submission by his Godly example.

- If a man neglects a persistent prayer life, he will never know how to walk with God in victory over the world, the flesh, and the devil. (Matthew 7:7-8). The men who pray and praise God every

149

day can be assured of God's special protection and power to defeat the forces of evil.

69. Crowns Given by God

- When you strive to do your best for God in all things, He will give you the incorruptible crown. (I Corinthians 9:25). The man who controls his spirit, his mouth, and his actions will receive this crown from the Lord.

- When you are presently loving the Lord and have the anticipation and long for His return, He will give you the crown of righteousness. (II Timothy 4:8). Every soldier in God's army has his own battles to fight, his own race to run; but if he stays true and looks for Jesus to come back for him, he receives a crown.

- When you love the Lord and continue serving Him in times of temptation without falling, you will be given the crown of life. (James 1:12). It is when you make it through life's temptations to victory that God gives the crown of life to all those who love Him.

- When you teach and preach the Word of God to the church, He gives you a crown of glory that fadeth not away. (I Peter 5:4). The most rewarding benefits are when you win the lost and feed the flock of God and then God gives you a crown that does not fade away.

- When you do not quit and keep walking by faith, no one can take your crown. (Revelation 3:11). We are tested and tried every day and if we keep on moving for God, He rewards persistence.

- When the right time comes, we will cast our crowns at Jesus' feet. (Revelation 4:10). It surely seems too good to be true that God Himself gives us the strength to fight all our battles and then rewards us for them.

70.   **The Heart is Wicked**

- Your heart is the center of all the days of your life. (Proverbs 4:23). Our hearts are like fountains of water that can give blessing or cursing to all those around us.

- Your heart is the source of how you act, what you think, and your spirituality. (Proverbs 23:7). Be very careful what you are thinking because thoughts become actions and actions turn into habits and habits become your life.

- It is your heart that lies, deceives, and misleads you and can take you to Hell. (Matthew 15:18). Destruction of a life flows from the mouth and is an indication of what your ears are hearing and what your eyes are seeing.

- It is what comes out of your mouth that tells what kind of heart you have. (Luke 6:45). It does not take very long to tell if a person has a Godly heart because his words will show you clearly the kind of person he is.

- No man can know how stubborn, how depraved, how desperate, wicked, and how deceitful our heart is. (Jeremiah 17:9). God is the only one who knows man's heart because He searches our heart and rewards us for good or for evil.

- Our heart is always the source of our covetousness and disbelief. (Hebrews 3:12; II Peter 2:14). Men seem to never be satisfied with

153

what they have and few are content, but God can give you Godliness with contentment.

- If you find yourself drawn to evil, know that it is your heart that draws you away from God and toward the world, the flesh, and the devil. Ask God to change your heart, cleanse your heart, and make it like He wants it to be.

- Do not trust your heart, but trust God instead. (Proverbs 3:5-6). Give every part of your heart to God holding no hidden places for yourself.

71. Pornography

- People of all ages have turned to the extremely addictive, sinful habit of pornography with its $15 billion revenue annually. The damage that has been done to our world through the internet has destroyed old and young alike. God have mercy on us.

- If you are addicted to pornography, ask God in prayer to deliver you with His power, and to cast down imaginations that do not agree with God's Word. (II Corinthians 10:35). The battle that all are in is who will you allow to occupy your heart and your mind. Will it be evil or will it be God?

- You must without fail stay away from all internet devices such as computers, video games, magazines, and anything where there is pornography. No matter how deep you are into this highly addictive trap of Satan, you can be delivered because it is still your choice what you will do.

- There are some sins so accepted in our society that you must find a pastor, counselor, or mature Christian who can help you hold yourself accountable for your thoughts and your actions. There are some habits that you will need outside help with to keep you accountable so be sure to seek Godly counsel.

- If you fall back into this sin, you must get Godly counsel and never allow yourself to stay down because of another failure, but get up again to fight the battle that rages in your mind. (Philippians 2:5). Ask God to help you review your mind and give you the mind of Christ found in His Holy Word.

- Above all, remember that you are not alone, but others can pray and help you get delivered. (I Corinthians 10:13). Get yourself a Godly support group from your church and with them claim the victory over sinful habits.

72. <u>Witchcraft</u>

- "Thou shall not suffer a witch to live." (Exodus 22:18). Our great God in His heart desires to protect His children from the terrible destruction of sin which is the reason for doing away with Satan's servants.

- Rebellion and stubbornness is considered by God to be the same as a witch and the same as idolatry, worthy of death. (I Samuel 15:23). If we are so filled with desire to do evil things that God is against, God will sometimes give what you long for as in the case with Saul.

- When a child was rebellious in the camp of the Hebrews, he was taken before the congregation and stoned to death. Without a speedy and serious penalty for sin, people continue thinking sin is all right to fool with.

- Confess your idolatry and stubbornness immediately to God and refuse to take into your heart this most hideous sin. (I John 1:9). Rebellion and stubbornness in our society now surrounds us, but God still has power to forgive those who come to Him.

- If you allow this kind of thinking to live inside of you, everything you do will be destroyed. Each of us has the power of choice inside of us to do what pleases God or do what pleases Satan.

- The most severe judgment of God is on the rebellious and stubborn soul whom God says He will reject. Men and women of earth have been deceived by the god of this world system for so long that they come to the place of no return.

- God says the way to deal with this kind of sin is to give your wicked heart to God. (Proverbs 23:26). For deliverance from these destructive ways, God asks us to give Him our hearts and focus our attention on His great love.

73. <u>The Unpardonable Sin</u>

- God's justice demands that sin be paid for. Because of God's justice, God sent His own Son to the cross of Calvary to pay the awful penalty for your sin and my sin.

- God does forgive the sinner, but He does not forgive the sin. Our sin has been paid for by the Blood of the Lamb of God so we could go free.

- God has put Jesus to death to pay for our sins. The kind of love God has for His people is so deep that we are unable to understand it until He opens our eyes and gives us glorified bodies.

- Our subject is the one sin that men do that cannot be forgiven. God's mercy is so great that He waits for all to repent of their sin and turn again back to God.

- You may have put off getting saved, even rejecting Christ, but that is not the unpardonable sin. The deceiver with his deception has convinced many that the pleasure of sin for a season is better than the rewards of righteousness.

- Not a single saved person can commit the unpardonable sin. When you confess your sin to God and invite Him into your heart to save you, God holds you in His hand where no one can take you from Him. (John 10:28).

- The unpardonable sin can only be committed by a sinner who knows the truth, but rejects the plea of the Holy Spirit and loses all desire to be saved. (Hebrews 6:4-6). The story is told about a lady who sat under the preaching of a great man of God for many years never responding to the Holy Spirit, but one day she found herself with no desire to be saved and it was too late.

74. The Holy Spirit as Our Personal Teacher

- God gave His people the Holy Spirit to teach us spiritual truths from the Holy Scripture. (Nehemiah 9:20). God has provided everything we could possibly need to live in His power victorious over the destructive forces of sin.

- It is the Holy Spirit who teaches what to say during times of preaching, teaching, and persecution. (Luke 12:12). God knows His children will want to prepare what they should say when persecuted, but God says I will tell you what you should say by my Spirit.

- The Holy Spirit is our comforter who teaches all things and helps us remember what God has said in His Word. (John 14:26). How beautiful it is to know that we have the sweet Holy Spirit who will teach us and bring memory of His Words to us at the right time.

- The Holy Spirit teaches us maturity by comparing spiritual things with the Spirit. Growing and becoming more mature in Christ is the marvelous work of God performed by His Holy Spirit.

- It is the Holy Spirit who set us apart from the world to do His will and His work. (I John 2:27). Let the Holy Spirit do His wonderful work in you preparing you for Heaven and instructing you how to please God.

- The Holy Spirit is the person who seals us with the seal of God so that we are His forever. (Ephesians 1:13). Those of us who are saved by His Blood are stamped with the seal of the Holy Spirit - God's guarantee there is nothing to fear.

- We know that we are the temple of God because He, the Holy Spirit, lives inside of us. (I Corinthians 3:16). I am His and He is mine and we walk together by the power of the Holy Spirit till I walk right into His glorious presence.

75. <u>How to Prepare for the Rapture</u>

- Watch for the trumpet sound when we which are alive and remain shall meet our Lord in the air. (I Thessalonians 4:16-18). Even the anticipation of the sure hope of His soon return keeps me singing and praising my Savior.

- After we meet the Lord in the clouds, we go to the Judgment Seat of Christ to give an account of everything we have done on Earth. (Romans 14:10-12). It is when you keep your thinking and your eyes on Jesus that you can be free to stop comparing yourself with those around you.

- When we stand before Jesus, our Savior, we will either be ashamed or approved and confident. (II Timothy 2:15). Definitely the most shameful thing that could ever take place would be when I shamefully stand before my God because I wasted my time on earthly pleasures.

- Be ready means be prepared to see Jesus any minute because He will come for His Bride soon. (Revelation 19:7). Whatever you do, be sure to give honor to the Lord of Glory for when He comes for us He will take us to Himself in marriage so get ready now.

- If we love His appearing, that love purifies us until He comes. (I John 3:2-3). With joy and delight to see our Savior face to face, he is coming back for His Bride.

- If we walk with God filled with the Spirit, we will come before Him in confidence. (I John 2:28). Readiness to meet our Savior is His desire for us because He loves to see His Bride live in peaceful confidence in Him.

76. Pride

- Pride in a person's heart means that soon destruction will come down on their head and they will fall. (Proverbs 16:18). By trusting God for everything in your life and humbling yourself under His mighty hand, we allow God to deliver us from falling.

- Strife always has someone who is its instigator, who stirs up other people, and God reminds us that it is sin. (Proverbs 28:25). It turns out to be an either/or decision that I can trust God or choose pride.

- All Egypt was destroyed after Pharaoh remained filled with pride. His pride cost him his son, his kingdom, and all his friends. (Exodus 5:2). The high cost of living selfish and prideful is clearly a life that is filled with failure and destruction.

- God warns us of pride, arrogance, conceit, and a haughty spirit that separates us from God's truth and all our co-workers and family friends. (Proverbs 16:18; Proverbs 8:13; Proverbs 26:12). Satan's pride cost him the highest position that was ever given by God.

- We are commanded to fear God, which leads us to hate evil, pride, and arrogance. (Proverbs 8:13). When you make fearing God your decision, you will hate evil ways, conceit, and a mouth filled with arrogance.

- When pride cometh, then cometh shame. (Proverbs 11:2). Pride has a little sister who follows him wherever he goes and ruins all his plans called shame.

- God tells us to humble ourselves and pray and seek God's face and turn from our wicked ways. (II Chronicles 7:14; I John 1:9). By choosing humility and prayer, we win the battle over wickedness and shame.

77. <u>Choosing the Right Church</u>

- Do not give your money to a liberal church where no souls are saved and the truth is not preached. By choosing the right church, you save yourself and your family from Satan's scheme to destroy us and our family.

- Do not listen to watered-down preaching from a version that is not the 1611 King James Bible. There are many churches where much of the Bible is not taught, not followed, and has too much of the world in them to make a difference.

- When you make a decision to join the church of your choice, it affects your eternity. When you choose a church because it is friendly or because of someone you know or because it is close to home, let me kindly say these are the wrong reasons.

- My church choice will change my own future and the future of my family, my friends, and my relatives. (Hebrews 10:25). Church is similar to marriage because you will become one with your choice whether right or wrong.

- By listening to a liberal preacher who stands for nothing, you will fall for anything. Your eternal future weighs in the balance depending on whether the preacher is bold enough to preach the whole counsel of God.

- Most of the world's churches are without Bible standards, without convictions about the truth, and are described by God as the commandments of men. (Matthew 15:9; II John 1:9-10). The road to Heaven never will be wide, broad, or easy, and most choose the easy, sinful road.

- Our world is filled with false teachers and false doctrine that our Lord teaches us to reject. (Mark 13:22). If you do not know church constitutions and bylaws, let me kindly suggest that you call an independent Baptist church office and ask the preacher to explain the vast difference in churches.

78. Proper Approach to Parents

- Make sure you have a thankful spirit. (I Thessalonians 5:18). The Bible tells us that with a thankful spirit you can live in the will of God.

- Be sure you have only encouraging words. No matter what the age, all those who encourage people are considered wise.

- Non-critical conversations show maturity. Mature Christians do not engage in gossip or critical language.

- Men think of others, while boys remain selfish. It is a rare person who looks for opportunities to give to others.

- You show spiritual growth by talking Bible truth. The best conversations you will have this side of Heaven will be about the Bible.

- Include your parents in your plans for the future. By talking to parents about your future, you add many years of wisdom to your life.

- Stay away from negative conversations. Some folks have a severe problem of seeing life with blinders over their eyes.

- When you are accused by others, say "I'm sorry." When you defuse a conversation with I'm sorry, you may win a friend.

- Avoid accusative, non-productive conversations. Wise people say fewer meaningless words than the foolish.

- When you hear bad news, do not respond immediately. By giving a quick answer to bad news, you usually will say something you don't mean.

- Learn the art of negotiation. Give into others when Bible truth is not the subject.

- Always speak with kindness politeness, and love. Those Christians with these qualities are few and lovely to be around.

- Apologize for anything you have done wrong. Learn the value of not arguing and apologizing.

- Give frequent compliments. Learn the language of encouragement and compliments.

- Make your time with your parents a time of peace and happiness. Controlled conversation with these topics will win friends.

- Remind your parents how much you love them and appreciate what they are doing for you. You can always find something nice to say if you are looking to be a blessing.

- Recall memories of when you and your family were happy working, playing, and laughing together. Family memories can be a place to visit in your mind for many years to come.

79. <u>First Steps in Climbing to Maturity</u>

Matthew 5:3

- I must empty myself of all selfish desire and realize that I need God's will, not my own will. The best prayer to God is when I ask Him to reveal in me sins of omission, sins of commission, and sins I am not aware of.

- When I admit that I need help and seek the help I need, I become a more mature Christian. Without God's constant help, I would have been gone from this Earth to pay for my sin in a burning Hell.

- Many there are who avoid showing weakness, avoid facing their need for help, and continue to fail through life, living in sin. God sends people into my life who can teach me, help me, instruct me, and pray for me. God is good.

- Pride and arrogance have a way of stopping us from crying out to God for help. Learn all you can from everyone you have in your life because they are sent by God to give you life's answers.

- By reaching out to others, you can turn all your problems into successes. Learn to love life by loving to learn more of God's Word and how to live it.

- Every lack inside of you can be used by God for good if you allow Him to rule your life. Every problem we face are only challenges put there by God so that we become overcomers for His glory.

- Humble yourself by admitting your need and becoming rich in the Kingdom of Heaven. Meekness and humility are those qualities of Jesus that we must follow if we plan to bring pleasure to God.

80. Great Men Follow Great Men

Jeremiah 5:5

- A wise man will search and find a great man of God and will work for him. Most men would have to admit that they set out on their own without learning how from the success of others.

- A great man will go as far as is necessary to find a great preacher and listen to him. Find the preacher who loves his people, loves soul winning, and separates himself from worldly pleasures.

- Great men of God have knowledge of God's Word, wisdom, God's power, and experience in the battles of the Christian life. Most Christians can tell when the preacher is inspired by God with messages from Heaven.

- God uses great men to change us so we can learn to seize opportunities that God places in front of us. It would be very wise to travel 50 miles one way to hear a great man of God move you to live Godly.

- Great men teach great truth from God's Holy Word and changes an ordinary man into a great man. Great truth from God's Word means the preacher is not afraid to preach on sin because it's Bible.

- Great preachers teach us how to live a supernatural life because they are living supernatural. No one should want what we might call an ordinary life, but all should want a supernatural life of miracles.

- You will be the same 10 years from now except for the people you choose to be part of your life and your choice of books you decide to read. Above all that you do in this life, be sure to choose your friends and your books wisely. The KJV Bible is always the right choice.

81. The Major Challenge for Teenagers

Psalm 40:6; Psalm 139:17; Psalm 103:1-5

- When you put your life of freedom and pleasure behind you God begins to bless you and promote you. Unsupervised teens who are addicted to this electronic generation will face difficult decisions.

- It is time to make permanent changes from childhood to adulthood. Children rely on parents to teach them how to stop being self-centered and learn to care about others, but that does not always take place.

- The past holds on to us and tries to pull us back into worldly practices. If you let your past rule your present, you will find your future destroyed also.

- Students who have trouble making the jump to adult life fight with thoughts of their past in which they had no responsibilities. It is when you cannot be trusted that no one will give you any responsible opportunities.

- Students are faced with a workload, a change in attitude, and how to become responsible for both words and actions. Those who have no work ethic and cannot control the mouth or their actions will be stalked by failure.

- This new life requires students to learn how to work. To get relationships with others is all we have on earth so treat others with respect and love and become successful.

- The new life that is offered to each student requires giving themselves to God and making plans to be His servant all the days of their life. If for any reason you are unable to surrender your heart to God, your reward from God will be greatly diminished.

- Those who make these changes will be rewarded by God for the rest of their life on Earth and in eternity. Only what has been done for Christ will last meaning that everything else will be burned up like wood, hay, and stubble at the Judgment Seat of Christ.

82. <u>Christian Manhood</u>

Matthew 4:19; Luke 2:52

- The way to leadership is first to be a good follower.

- Only good followers are used of God to be leaders.

- If you want God to take care of you, be sure to take special care of others.

- In God's Kingdom, the first shall be last and the last shall be first.

- The way up is down. Before you get saved, you must admit that you are a hopelessly lost sinner.

- The way down is up in God's Kingdom. You must humble yourself under the mighty hand of God before He will exalt you in His own time.

- It is when you spend quality time on your knees praying that God will give you an influence in the lives of many.

- The preparation years are far more important than the years doing the jobs you prepared for.

- The longer the preparation, the greater your effectiveness for God will be.

- If you change yourself and get out of school too soon because you were impatient, your success will be short lived.

- Time spent in prayer and on your knees and in God's Word in the night hours gives you something to give to others in the daytime.

- The greatest person in God's Kingdom is the pastor who gave his life to God with a servant's heart here on Earth.

- The beauty of each day on Earth is in praising and thanking God for His mercy that He loved us enough to let us pass onto others His love for them. "In everything give thanks, for this is the will of God in Christ Jesus concerning you." (I Thessalonians 5:18).

- The beauty of living is always in the giving because what you keep for yourself you can have, but what you give away you keep forever.

83. Three Most Subtle Deceptions by Satan Today

God's Word – Churches - Music

- Satan has used the printing press to deceive this world with a multitude of erroneous versions of the Bible. (Revelation 22:18-19); Matthew 4:4; Psalm 199:89; Psalm 12:6-7; Matthew 5:18; Revelation 1:3). The deception is so strong that many of God's people find it hard to believe that the King James Version is preserved for us from Heaven when God spoke His Holy Word.

- Since the church at Jerusalem, there has been a departure from the truth that is so strong that today most Christians do not know how to make a Godly choice for going to a church where they can be sure the truth is preached and taught. As difficult as it may seem, each Christian is held responsible for knowing enough Bible truth to make his choice with knowledge and wisdom.

- Music was created by God for praise and worship. (Ephesians 5:19; Colossians 3:16; I Corinthians 14:33; I Corinthians 14:40; II Corinthians 11:13-15; Ezekiel 28:15). When songwriters put Christian words to music they like because of its timing like rock, pop, and contemporary, it does not make it Godly music.

- The amount of damage and destruction Satan has done by deceiving this world will never be realized until the Great White Throne Judgment.

179

May God have mercy on those who have gone after the world, the flesh, and the devil.

• God warns us many times in His Word not to be deceived. (Matthew 24:4; I Corinthians 6:9; Galatians 6:7; Ephesians 5:6; II Thessalonians 2:3; I John 3:7). The strongest and most severe deception comes on this world's population prior to the Lord's return.

84. <u>Choose Your Battles</u>

(Ephesians 6:12; I Timothy 6:12; II Corinthians 10:4; II Timothy 2:4)

- The Christian battle is not a physical battle, but a spiritual battle. If you want to win the battle, you will have to control your thoughts and change those thoughts into God's thoughts, His Holy Word.

- Losers in God's army will fight each other. One of the most disturbing actions of God's people is when they begin to turn on each other and fight each other.

- Losers think they must at all cost defend themselves. The natural tendency is to think you must defend yourself, but God reserves the right to defend His children.

- Satan's priority is to cause God's people to fight each other. We are here to encourage to build and to love each other no matter how it looks or feels to us.

- The spiritual battle that we are in belongs to the Lord. (I Samuel 17:47; Psalm 23:8; I Samuel 18:17; Psalm 50:15). When you choose to fight your battles alone without God, you will always be defeated.

- When we take matters into our own hands, we will lose. We are not equipped or strong enough to win against the powers of darkness.

- Pick and choose your battles carefully if you want to win them. Some battles that we think are ours are not anything to pursue or get involved in so pray and win.

- We must choose when, where, and how to fight with God's power, not our own power. The Bible says power belongeth unto our Lord so use wisdom to know when to get involved and when to just give it to God.

- We have no power of our own to fight without completely relying on God's Word. Know the Word of God well and use God's Word wisely to fight all your spiritual battles.

- A large amount of our battles are won when we have God's given peace in our heart and realize that God is in charge. (Philemon 4:6-7). When the children of God went to Him in prayer and fasting, He fought for them and defeated their enemies.

85. <u>Secular University or College</u>

- The philosophy of these colleges is always and forever anti-God. Many of our colleges and universities in our past were started by Godly presidents and teachers whose purpose was to draw close to God.

- The philosophy of our nation's universities is anti-American. The truth about our country's beginnings has been hidden from modern students for so many years that few want to protect our nation.

- The professors will definitely use every avenue available to them to convince you to change or rethink your Christian point of view. At this point, even our high schools have persecuted students for pursuing the truth about God.

- The pressure is on all who are saved to join the crowd concerning your convictions, concerning evolution, ISIS, Islamic ideas, and all ungodly philosophies. While our teachers embrace all other religions around the world, it becomes against the law to stand for truth.

- You will face unbelievable persecution to compromise your convictions about the opposite sex in a co-ed environment where anything goes. If you want to stay pure for God's glory and keep yourself unspotted from the world, attend a Godly school, not the ungodly one.

- These philosophies are so powerfully entrenched that if you are able to graduate without losing your core beliefs, it will be miraculous. God have mercy on our schools in this country where we no longer hear anyone pray out loud and read our Bibles in the classroom because it is not allowed.

86. Contentment

- Godliness with contentment is a very powerful combination that brings us great and mighty blessings from God. (I Timothy 6:6). God made all of His children different and unique so if you want contentment, you will need to stop comparing yourself with others.

- I must confess my sin and learn to forgive myself and forgive others. Satan's goal for us is to live in stress and worry about things we cannot change or do anything about.

- I must resist the urge to be self-centered and absorbed in my own thoughts, problems, and needs. The quickest way to stop being so self-absorbed is to find someone in need and find a way to help them.

- I must learn to be content in whatever conditions I find myself in. (I Timothy 6:8). God's plans are not always clear to us because He wants us to stop trying to figure out life without Him.

- I must require of myself contentment in what I have been given by God. It is said that men are never satisfied, but always wanting more. If that is your condition, confess your sin to God.

- The things in this world like money, fame, and position can rob of God's gift of contentment. (Proverbs 15:16). We are literally flooded with schemes and advertisements to make us want more than we need, but God's promise is to supply need.

- God wants me to be happy, satisfied, and content with the job we have been given and the income He provides. (Luke 3:14). God have mercy on us who live in such a materialistic world where we seem to forget how to live simply.

- Contentment is given to those Christians who decide they will seek God and go after being content with what God has given to them. The requirement today is the same as in Jesus' day when His solution was continual thanksgiving for everything.

- To be content is to be in rest in your mind; quiet satisfaction of mind concerning any condition or event that comes into my life. You will come closer to a life of Godliness and contentment after you completely offer yourself to God by the renewing of mind every day. (Romans 12:2).

87. <u>Depression</u>

- When you are anxious, worried, or stressed, your thoughts are on yourself which means you are leaving out of your life God's Word. Drugs, alcohol, pills, and psychiatrists will never deliver us from the stresses of this life.

- When you decide to live by faith and apply God's Word to your present state of mind, the facts change your mind on how you see trouble. (Psalms 34:14). The strength and power of our God is seen and verified when He uses even our weaknesses to His advantage for our benefit.

- All Christians have trouble in this world with their old nature and their past life. The constant war that goes on inside of us is similar to war that is all around us, but God delivers us when we make Him our constant Shepherd.

- If you decide to win against the old nature and do what Jesus did to Satan in Matthew 4:4, you will use God's Word in every trial and become a victor for God's glory. Think the Words of God in your heart, speak His Word with your mouth, and use God's powerful words for complete deliverance just like Jesus.

- In Philippians we learn that to forget our wicked past and focus on our bright future we can win the prize that God wants to give us. (Philippians 3:13-14). Every child of God must focus their attention on a marvelous, bright future when we will all be changed into our glorified bodies in our New Jerusalem forever.

- God tells us it is wrong to allow our worries about our present troubles to take from us the peace we are given when we thank God for everything. (Philippians 4:6-7). Available to all of us is a life of love, joy, peace, and rest that this world knows nothing about.

- Depression can be turned into praise by a decision to transform your mind by letting God renew your thoughts with His holy and powerful truth. (Romans 12:2).

88. The Value of My Word

Ecclesiastes 5:2

- The wisdom of this verse is that if you speak less words in your life on Earth you will have less to answer to God for at the judgment. God hears and records all of our words, good or bad, sad or mad, so if you speak less words you have less to answer to God for.

- God requires accountability of every word that comes out of your mouth. It would be much wiser to be slow to answer people because you chose your words and spoke them in wisdom rather than haste.

- Words become your life here on Earth. What men do in this life comes from the words they have learned either in school or in books or in the Bible.

- A person who knows the Bible is aware that less words are going to be a blessing to yourself and all who know you. (Proverbs 17:27). God wants us to use carefully chosen words that honor and glorify Him so that He can reward His children.

- Those who speak a multitude of unwise words will find that this evil comes from your heart. (Matthew 5:37). Man's tongue is an unruly evil and must be tamed like a wild animal and restrained from wickedness and evil.

- When a man walks with God, he will want to bring peace to all who hear him. If you want to know how to encourage friends and please God with your life, speak more of God's Word and less of your own words.

- From our words we offend people or we can encourage people. The person who offends people with unkind words usually has a bad spirit, a bad temper, and a bad habit.

- If we love like God loves, we can impact others with sweet words that heal the hearts of hurting people. (Ephesians 4:32). If you have a desire to, you can be a refreshing fragrance to all those who know you by your choice of your loving, forgiving, and kind words.

89. <u>Scheduling My Life for God's Glory</u>

Matthew 6:33

- By scheduling the Kingdom of God and His righteousness in my life and in my daily activities, I will receive God's promise that He will take care of all my needs. God's plans are all perfect and His timing is right on schedule so learn from His example and receive all that you need.

- When we learn to schedule, we will not be making wrong choices that can ruin our walk with God. It is when you have to make too many everyday choices that you will make unwise decisions that cause your failure.

- The wise Christian lets his schedule keep him in Kingdom blessings. There is a way to live in God's Kingdom that will keep you from falling if in your schedule God is always first.

- Many Christians forfeit the promises of God because they continually make unwise choices. Usually unwise choices are due to a lack of Bible knowledge and wisdom.

- The reason I must take away my choices is to ensure I live by the Godly schedule I made for myself which becomes my success story. All success stories where Godly men and women have risen above the rest is due to a life of sacrifice and planning and hard work.

- Take your Godly living to a new, higher level when you live by God's Word because it is in your schedule. No one who studies, reads, or memorizes Scripture will be the same because it always and without fail takes you to a higher spiritual level than you were.

- I will thank God and praise Him as my new schedule becomes my protection from this world. If you let it, this world will keep you busy in trivialities and non-essentials stealing your time from God.

- It is what you do first that sets the priorities where God wants them helping you to win the battles each day. Take inventory of how much of your life is spent on yourself and how much time you give to God's Word, prayer, and praising.

- Choose God first in everything you do and watch Him open the doors of Heaven and pour out such a large blessing that you hardly have enough room to receive it. Your first thoughts in the morning need to be thankful to God and praising Him and loving Him. If not, make it so.

- Put in your schedule soulwinning, loving others, being kind to others, and singing to keep up your good attitude. (Colossians 3:16). Find a Christian who has a sweet, humble spirit and you will hear that person singing and praising God all the day long.

90. <u>Living Peaceful and Calm</u>

- When you make a decision to love and make peace with everyone, your heart and your spirit will follow. (Proverbs 16:3).

- By focusing on peace and quiet, you can increase your ability to study and meditate with great success. (Psalm 1:1-3).

- The person who has calmed his spirit is known by others as one who can be trusted. (Psalm 119:165).

- If you get control of your actions, you can have the fruit of the spirit. (Galatians 5:22).

- In a world of stressed out people, it takes effort on your part to avoid being pulled into a critical and judgmental spirit. (Matthew 7:1-5).

- By learning to be peaceful and calm, you can go through troubles and stressful times without being disturbed. (Isaiah 26:3). Each child of God has a main mission issued by God to treat everyone God gives to us with lovingkindness, forgiveness, and tenderheartedness. (Ephesians 4:32).

- As a child of God, you can have God's love by practicing loving others. Practice joy and you can have joy. Practice peace and you can have peace. Practice kindness and you can have kindness. Practice patience and you can have patience. If you have love for people, those people will feel loved by you. (Proverbs 16:3).

- It is truly difficult to comprehend how God could love sinners who hate Him, mock Him, spit in His face, and ridicule Him all their life.

- Perhaps one of the most difficult tasks in this life is to love people who have less character than we do and cause us extreme heartache and many troubles.

- Those Christians who continue to love others and choose to go through the struggles with them will have lived more like God than all the rest of us.

- The love of God is truly what this world needs and what we need from each other.

91.   The Place of Promise for You!

- God promised the Jews a place called the Promise Land. This place would include a land of their own, descendants so many they could not be numbered, and blessings far too many to describe.

- The land and the seed and the blessing would be dependent on the Jews trusting God and claiming this land for their own - the very place called Canaan Land.

- The spiritual blessings in your future are waiting for you at the location where God is going to pour out His richest treasures if you go to the right place.

- There is a place God wants you to go where God will bless you far beyond your fondest dreams. (Genesis 12:7; Genesis 13:15-18).

- What decisions will you make, what direction will you take, what things will you give up in this world to find that one place where God gives you your Canaan Land of promise.

- Find your earthy heritage by yielding your will to God trusting in His plan to take you to that place of blessing.

- Do not allow anyone or anything on earth to rob you of God's power, God's presence, and God's promises at the place prepared for you here in

195

Earth and in Heaven. (Hebrews 2:1; Hebrews 4:1; Hebrews 10:35).

92. <u>How to Find a True Friend</u>

Look for a true friend for yourself.

- A true friend will love you like God loves you for who you are, not what you can do for them. (Proverbs 7:17).

- When you find a true friend, you will notice that he or she lives Bible truth.

- A true friend will love and accept you no matter what struggles you are going through.

- A Godly true friend will always tell you the truth that comes from God, not from this world.

- A true friend is that special person God sent into your life to teach you things you would not pick up any other way. (I John 1:7).

- A Godly sent true friend will always make you a better person than you thought possible. (Proverbs 27:17).

- If you find one true friend in your lifetime, you will have found a Godly person more valuable to you than all the gold in this world.

- That one true Godly friend that God brings into your life will pray for you and change your future forever. (Acts 2:42; Phil. 1:3).

- Jesus calls us His friends, and how He could call sinners His friends is so wonderful that I cannot fully comprehend it.

- If you can understand that Jesus has made you His friend, you can also know that He will in your life send people to you to love and be loved by them.

93. <u>Preserve Life</u>

Genesis 45:5

- My mission on earth is to preserve life because life is God's gift to me and my greatest treasure to pass on to others.

- Notice that a large number of people in this world system criticize, tear down, and destroy each other's life.

- I can preserve life when I use my mouth to give the words of life, the Living Word of God. (Matthew 4:4).

- God sent Joseph into this world for a very specific purpose of keeping his own family alive during a very severe famine. (Genesis 45:5).

- God has sent us into this world also to preserve precious life.

- The question we must ask ourselves is are we destroying the lives of others or are we preserving the lives of those around us?

- By your speech and your spirit, you either preserve or destroy others.

- If you love people and forgive, you can preserve the lives of those in your family and your friends.

- If you are angry, critical, and judgmental, your own actions and words are tearing apart the people God has given you to encourage and bless.

- The damage some people are inflicting on their family and friends is extremely hurtful to their hearts, their emotions, and affects them the rest of their life.

- The pain and anguish that comes from angry, unforgiving people is often passed on from generation to generation.

- What affect are you having on those around you? Is it destruction or preservation?

94. <u>Living in the Kingdom of God While Residing in Satan's World System</u>

The Kingdom of God

- You can decide to live above the fighting, above the wickedness, above the competition for game and money by transforming your mind. Transformation takes replacing worldly thoughts with Kingdom thoughts that are written in the Living Word of God. (Romans 12:2).

- While you are driving you can sing; while you are working you can praise; and while you are talking to people you can be loving. What a way to live above and beyond the normal mindset of greed and hate in this world. (Colossians 3:16).

- If you are experiencing the power of being filled with the Spirit of God, you are living above the influence and deception of Satan's lies.

- Jesus teaches us that His Kingdom is not that which comes from this world, but His Kingdom is from above. (John 18:36; Colossians 3:1-2).

- When it is your heart's desire to be heavenly minded, you will begin to have power over the attacks of Satan.

- We can live in the Kingdom of God while residing in Satan's world by focusing our heart and mind on our Savior and His will.

- Kingdom thoughts come from the Living Word of God, while Satanic thoughts come from our old nature and our past life of sin.

95. <u>The Magnificent Love of God</u>

- The love of God is so glorious and powerful and wonderful and beautiful in our eyes. With God's love, we are spared from hate, from wickedness, from failure, from disaster, and from Hell. (John 3:16).

- Love is not what God does, but who God is and means to us that He will always be true to Himself on our behalf. (I John 4:8).

- If you are having trouble loving others with your heart and your words, you need to bathe yourself in the Living Word of God. (I John 4:8).

- When you desire a change in your view of the circumstances that surround your life, nothing in this world is more life changing than when you began giving to others God's miraculous gift of love that He has given to you.

- God's love for us is certain no matter what His children do or do not do. His love never changes and He tells us His love for us is everlasting. (Jeremiah 31:3).

- In our troubled world that is our mission field we must love all people God sends into our life. I can change my world through the power of loving everyone I meet. (John 13:34-35).

- When God commands us to love Him, that command is given to us because of His love and for our eternal blessings that He is waiting to pour out on those who have chosen to love Him. (Proverbs 10:12).

96. <u>Victory Over My Guilty Past</u>

Philippians 3:13-14; Luke 9:62

- Our God who forgives us according to His promise in I John 1:9 wants us to forget our guilty past.

- If your guilt seems to persist, it may help you to write down on paper what it is that is giving you grief.

- Take that paper and tear it in tiny pieces to put it in a secure garbage can.

- By placing it in the garbage in pieces, it can be a way of disposing of your guilty past.

- The act of doing this can be a way of closing the door to your guilty past and your sinful habits.

- Each time these guilty thoughts persist or come back to defeat you, verbally out loud ask God to remove them from your thoughts.

- Claim in prayer the Blood of Jesus over your heart and mind. (Phil. 4:6-8).

- Forget your sinful past and decide to move forward without looking back. (Luke 9:62).

97.   <u>The Riches That God Offers His Children</u>

- God offers us riches far beyond what our minds can grasp and His offer is for all mankind. (Romans 2:4; Luke 19:10).

- The riches our loving God is referring to are numerous gifts that can only be received by seeking to know our God through over 8,000 promises found in the Living Word of God.

- It is amazing how that insignificant man could be so filled with pride that he would tell the God who made him I am too busy to receive your riches of goodness to me.

- The goodness of God is everywhere you look, everywhere you go, and farther than your eyes can see. Open your heart to God and He will open your eyes to see life surrounded by the goodness of God. (Psalm 107:8, 15, 21, 31).

- When you open your eyes each morning your sleep is God's gift, the air you breathe is God's air, the dirt or floor you stand on is from God, as well as every member of your family is a gift of God's riches offered to you.

- God's riches offered to us are in the form of undeserved favor called the grace of our loving Savior who gave His life for man.

- God's blood is offered to you to cleanse you from all your sin and wickedness so that you can be His own purchased possession for all eternity.

- In Psalm 103, God offers to forgive all your iniquities and heal all your diseases, buy back your life from destruction, and then crown you with His lovingkindness and His tender mercies.

- In Galatians 5, God wants us to receive love, joy, peace, longsuffering, gentleness, goodness, faith, meekness, and temperance, and much more for the child who would be willing to give himself to God.

- God invites us to experience, taste, and even to see His goodness and His riches that are waiting for the child of God to receive from Him.

98. <u>Trouble Common to All</u>

- Temptations, trouble, and struggles are an important part of life that all men will face, but it is how you receive these things that either make you bitter or make you better.

- If you find that you have no temptations or troubles, check and see if you are still alive.

- When you find yourself angry at others, disappointed in others, and often critical, know that you are severely lacking in spiritual power.

- Your spiritual power to handle each day's challenges comes from your connection with God whose power is freely given to His children who ask for it.

- The things to check when lacking in God's power would be your closeness to God, your praise time, and your prayer time.

- While all of us will be tested each day we live, it is not to take us down but designed by God to lift us up as we rely on Him.

- God is so good to us in developing our walk with Him that His highest plan for our life is to benefit and get stronger with each new trial.

- God can use evil in this world for testing His children in every hidden corner of our heart.

- The question we must ask ourselves is how are we responding to our evil world and those who give us difficult problems with their bad spirits.

- There are many unseen spiritual powers we cannot see that only our close walk with God can get the victory we so desire.

99. <u>Learn to Give</u>

- It is what you give to others that God will allow you to keep; it is what you keep selfishly for yourself that you cannot have.

- All of us want happy days in which we are pleased with God, pleased with ourselves, and happy to be around others.

- You will never find happiness by seeking happiness by itself, but happiness is a byproduct of making others happy and making others feel good about themselves.

- By giving out forgiveness to others, you will find forgiveness for yourself; by giving peace to others, peace will be yours to enjoy.

- When you encourage others in their life struggles, you will find encouragement comes to your heart.

- If you look for someone in need and give that person what they need, when you get back home God promises He will take care of all your needs.

- There is no greater joy in life than to give like God gives to you even His only Son so that we can know that we have been given everlasting life.

- When you become a giving person, you have become more like God than most of this world's people would understand.

- Remember that it is what you keep that you cannot have, but what you give you will keep forever.

- Your greatest achievement will be when you finally give everything you have to God and as much as you can to others.

100. <u>Making Praise My Priority</u>

- We find that our Lord longs for His children to praise Him for His goodness and His wonderful works to the children of men. (Psalm 107:8, 15, 21, 31).

- God won the war for His people after they began to sing and to praise the Lord. How many battles could we have won if only we were in the powerful habit of singing and praising God.

- After the Red Sea closed its waters on Pharaoh and all his army, Israel sung songs of praise, thanksgiving, and gave God the glory for protecting His people.

- Many Scripture references have Israel praising and giving thanks together and singing about the goodness of God.

- David understood the tremendous power and presence of God when he said, "I will praise thee, O Lord, with my whole heart. I will be glad and rejoice in thee: I will sing praise to thy name, O thou Most High." (Psalm 9:1-2).

- The best and most successful time of prayer to God will be experienced after you have had a season of thanksgiving and praise to God.

101. <u>Can I Live in God's Will – The Most Powerful Way to Live</u>

- The question most Christians would fail to answer correctly would be how can I be sure I am living in God's will?

- When you find yourself losing your battles and going backward, the first place to look is what is coming out of your mouth most of your day?

- Decide to record how many times you make a negative statement or verbalize a complaint about the weather, or gripe to your mate, or disapprove of what someone said.

- It may seem to be a small error to you and I, but it means we are carrying a bad spirit.

- By being accountable for what comes out of your mouth each time you open your lips, you may be able to experience staying in the will of God.

- We are invited by God to give thanks for everything all day long, no matter how things turn out or how we see it.

- It's interesting that almost everything we face tries to take from us the thankful spirit that is God's requirement for staying in His will. (I Thessalonians 5:18).

- We are kept from experiencing the will of God by our evil heart and our uncontrolled tongue. We are being robbed of the blessing of God's will because most Christians have not yielded their spirit and tongue to God on the altar.

- Now we know why so many Christians fight each other instead of fighting the devil.

- It makes it clear to us why many have such a struggle with sin.

- Until we completely surrender our bad spirit to God, His will is still His for us, but not ours for Him.

- As quick as you can get in the beautiful habit of thanking God for everything whether it seems good or bad, just give thanks and stay in God's perfect will and enjoy the journey of life God's way.

102. <u>My Attitude is Powerful</u>

Isaiah 40:31; Galatians 5:22

- People will see you precisely as you see yourself.

- With a negative attitude, those around you will treat you negatively.

- With a Godly attitude, people will see you in their minds as Godly.

- If you want to have success in your Christian life, respond to others as successful and they will treat you like you are successful.

- God will pour His richest blessings on that man who reaches higher and higher for spiritual truth in His Holy Word.

- Your attitude about life can discourage everyone around you or can call those same people to seek our God.

- If you do not have an overflowing love for God, you will not be able to pass on to anyone what you do not possess.

- If there is deep-seated anger in your heart that you have not sufficiently dealt with under stress, it will raise its ugly head again.

- In some cases if a person is demon oppressed, he must claim the Blood of Jesus and surrender

215

his heart, mind, and body to God in prayer in order to be delivered.

- Complete surrender and total yielding is the substance that overcoming victory over sin is made of.

- No one who holds on to any amount of sin or rebellion will ever know and experience the mighty power of God that comes through the holiness of God.

- Those who give God everything will experience God's presence and His love in a way that others will not understand even while living among them.

- Attitude that is not derived from God's Word means you are serving Satan while you are serving self.

- Will you pass on a Godly attitude or a Satanic attitude?

103. <u>The First Priority for All Children</u>

Ephesians 6:1-3; Mark 7:10; Proverbs 20:11; Deuteronomy 6:6-9

- Nothing in all the Bible is more valuable and important for children than to obey and honor their parents.

- Those who honor and obey are given a promise from God that will bring into their life great joy and reward each day they live.

- God always follows through with His promises and this one is for children who Jesus loves dearly.

- It brings a pleasure to God to prepare a life of quality and power with God and power with men for that one who takes God at His promise and runs with it.

- The most valuable lesson parents could teach children is that of obedience and honor so that the way they take will already be prepared by God for success.

- Far too many parents who do not obey God themselves or honor their Creator, weaken the life of their children with wickedness and destruction.

- Children learn to obey and honor God by learning these everlasting truths from Godly parents.

- This is the life of spiritual beauty that comes from generations of parents who hand God's truth down to their children's children.

- Those parents who have believed God's promises and lived them as well as taught them to their children will be rewarded for all eternity with generations of their children in Heaven with them forever.

- Nothing is more rewarding to a grandfather than to see his children teach their children how to obey and honor authority bringing spiritual blessings to all.

- Those children who were not blessed with spiritual parents can start a magnificent life of spiritual quality if they would believe God and put into everyday practice honor and obedience of their parents.

- It is never too late to take God up on His promises in His Word and watch what He will do for you and your children.

- A long life of health and spiritual wealth is waiting for you when you put into practice each day God's marvelous promises.

- Saving your children and generations to come from a life of pain on earth and Hell for eternity is what Ephesians 6 is teaching us because God loves everyone, even you.

ABOUT THE AUTHOR

I was age 12 when God called me into the ministry. Looking back I realize it was a commitment totally by faith. I rode my bicycle to church until we moved away and then a youth director would pick me up for youth activities and church.

After graduation from Hughson Union High School I went to Modesto Junior College for one year of electronics. On my 18th birthday I took the bus to Oakland to take the oath for the US Navy. The Navy made me a radioman, working in communications. Four years later I was given an honorable discharge.

God led me to Cedarville University in Cedarville, Ohio and I graduated 4 years later with a pre-seminary Bible major. I still felt I needed some practical training and went to Hyles Anderson College in Crown Point, Indiana. While at the Hammond Baptist Church in Indiana, I was called by James Clemensen to pastor the Willows Baptist Church in Willows, California.

During my 53 years in the ministry, 7 churches called me to be their pastor. Four of those churches were in California, my home state. Three of those churches were in New York, 2 of which God helped me to start. I pastored the Hall Street Baptist Church in Marysville for 16 years and was called to Agape Boarding School in Stockton, MO to counsel boys whose parents needed help.

I currently preach chapel messages to the boys and counsel them 5 days a week. It was in those counseling sessions that the Holy Spirit gave me the book, *Chosen For Deliverance*.

My wife Patricia has been beside me in the ministry over 24 years through all the trials of the pastorate.

I give glory to God for allowing me and my wife to be in his army, winning battles and praising God for His mercy and his grace.

CPSIA information can be obtained
at www.ICGtesting.com
Printed in the USA
LVHW080328190322
713650LV00001B/1